JOHN KNOX.

"He who never feared the face of man." p. 173.

SKETCHES

OF THE

PRESBYTERIAN CHURCH,

CONTAINING

A BRIEF SUMMARY OF ARGUMENTS IN FAVOUR OF ITS PRIMITIVE AND APOSTOLIC CHARACTER

AND

A VIEW OF ITS PRINCIPLES, ORDER, AND HISTORY,

DESIGNED ESPECIALLY FOR THE

YOUTH OF THE CHURCH.

BY THE

REV. J. E. ROCKWELL.

PHILADELPHIA:
PRESBYTERIAN BOARD OF PUBLICATION,
NO. 1334 CHESTNUT STREET.

CONTENTS.

PREFACE.

The following work, first commenced with the simple hope of rendering more attractive and useful the pages of the Sabbath-school Visitor, where it originally appeared in the form of letters to children, has been carefully re-written, and enlarged by important additions. The design of the writer has been to supply, as far as possible, a want which has been greatly felt, of some suitable history of the Presbyterian Church, to be placed especially in the hands of our youth.

He has sought to group together the facts by which that history can be traced up, not simply to the Reformation, but to the Apostolic age, and to the type of a pure and primitive Christianity. He has desired to make familiar to the mind, the rise, progress, struggles, and successes of the great principles of Presbyterianism, and to set forth their influence upon the Church and the world.

In addition to the ordinary works of reference, he would acknowledge his indebtedness to the researches of Drs. Smyth and Hodge of our own Church, and Dr. Hetherington of the Church of Scotland, whose valuable contributions to the cause of Presbyterianism have nobly illustrated and defended its order and doctrines.

While other denominations are claiming for themselves the authority of antiquity, and in some instances denying to us even the name and character of a Church of Christ, it is well that our youth should be put on their guard against the fascinations of such assumptions, and made to understand that the principles in which they have been educated, were not first developed at the Reformation, but were the *essential elements of the Apostolic Church,* and that through all the darkness of Papal night, there were Christian communities who held intrinsically the same order, which, at the Reformation, was *resumed in its important features in every Reformed Church, but that of England.*

This volume is now sent forth, with the prayer that it may be useful in establishing the minds of our youth, and in leading them to love the distinctive doctrines which form the strength and glory of the Israel of God. J. E. R.

CHAPTER I.

INTRODUCTORY.

THE design of the following pages is to present an outline of the history and principles of the Presbyterian church, and to set forth in a condensed and yet sufficiently explicit form, the facts which show its doctrines and order to be primitive and apostolic. It is no part of this purpose to teach *that it is the only true church, out of which there is no salvation,* or to make invidious comparisons between it and other branches of the family of Christ.

A sincere and zealous attachment to the doctrines and order of the church with which we are connected by birth and education, or as the result of our earnest convictions of truth, may exist with the most liberal and enlarged friendship for all who, though differing from us in many of their religious views, still bear the image of Christ. We profess to be only a branch of his family; a part of that great army which, though divided into sections, has one leader, and is engaged in a conflict with sin and error, under one glorious banner. Yet, while no particular denomination of Christians has any claim to be called, by way of eminence *the church*, it is evident that some one of them approaches nearer than others to the apostolic model, and embodies the general features of the first Christian community. In the gradual departure from the faith once delivered to the saints, which at length assumed the form of Popery, and introduced the "Man of Sin," the church lost its original simplicity and purity, until the Reformation again restored the truths of the gospel to their appropriate place, and threw off the dreadful load of superstition and error that had for ages rested upon the minds of men. At that period, the Protestant church assumed the general features by which it is now distinguished. While in their views of the prominent and cardinal truths of our holy religion, the Reformers were agreed, they differed in regard to external arrangements and forms of government. Those differences still exist, and their prominent characteristics are set forth in the names which the various Christian denominations of the world now bear.

The Episcopal church maintains an order of prelates, having office and power distinct from the ministry, and superior to it, who alone are able to ordain, and to whom is committed the especial oversight and care of all the churches found within their appointed districts. At the Reformation this form of government was only regarded as essential to the *perfection* of the church, while it was not denied that true churches *might exist* without it. Since then the idea has been advocated, and widely received, that the order of prelates obtain their power by a direct succession from the apostles, whose representatives they are, and that no ministry can be valid which is not received by their ordination, and that there can be no salvation out of the pale of the church thus organized. Thus, while the articles of faith, as received by that denomination, and faithfully preached by many of its clergy, are purely evangelical, dogmas are maintained by others of the same connection, which if true would abolish the doctrine that we are saved through faith, and blot out the hopes of multitudes who are leading consistent and holy lives, though they have never been united with that branch of the church of Christ.

The Congregationalists wholly differ from these views. They maintain that the ministers of the gospel have equal power and authority, and that the discipline and government of the church is vested in the people forming a particular congregation, who are independent of all other organizations, and in whom all power originates.

The Presbyterian form of government assumes that a particular congregation is only part of the church, to which it is responsible, and that authority hath been vested in its ministers and officers, who constitute its courts, and by whom its discipline is administered. It agrees with Congregational churches in asserting the equality of the ministry, but differs from them in their views of the independency of each congregation. It agrees with the Episcopal church in its maintaining a union of many congregations under one episcopacy, but differs from it in vesting that oversight in the hands of the Presbytery, composed of several Bishops of equal authority, and not of a prelate of power superior to the rest.

This form of government, we sincerely believe, approaches the nearest to that first instituted by the apostles. The Lord Jesus Christ, as the supreme Head of the church, has alone the right and authority to decree its laws, and to institute its ministry. As such a head he appointed special and extraordinary officers, who were first to be witnesses to his death and resurrection, and *then* to arrange the church in accordance with the great principles he had established. These officers were called apostles, who attested the truth of their mission by many signs and miracles which God did through them. They had no successors in the apostolic office. They could have none, in the very nature of the case. When Judas had lost his place as an apostle, by his transgression, and it was deemed essential to keep the number of apostles complete, one was chosen from the number of those who had personally known Christ, and was ordained to be a *witness of his resurrection.* See Acts i. 22. When these witnesses were all dead, the apostolic office ceased. We are nowhere told that they appointed any successors. They could not. But it was necessary that the church should be *instructed* and *governed.* And hence, Presbyters or Elders were appointed, some of whom were to preach, while others were to assist in the government of the church. Thus Paul says to Timothy, "The things that thou hast heard of me, the same commit thou unto faithful men who may be able to *teach* others also." It was the *doctrine* of the apostles which was to have a succession, and not their *office.* The men whom they appointed as officers were *Elders.* Thus in Acts xiv. 23, it is said, "When they had ordained them *Elders* in every church." And in Titus i. 5, we read, "For this cause left I thee in Crete; that thou shouldst set in order the things that are wanting, and ordain *Elders* in every city as I had appointed thee." And the apostles gave them counsel and advice only as Presbyters. Thus Peter says, 1 Peter v. 1, "The Elders which are among you I exhort, who also am an Elder." These officers are called by different names, according to the duties laid upon them. The words Bishop and Pastor are applied to those who preach the word, and have an especial watch over the flock, and administer the ordinances of the house of God. Others who rule, but do not preach, are called "helps and governments." Thus in 1 Timothy v. 17, it is said, "Let the elders that rule well be accounted worthy of double honour, especially they who *labour* in word and doctrine." But we nowhere read that any church was under the care of a *single* Elder, or that one Presbyter was elevated in *office* above others.

The word Bishop is only another expression applied to the office of Elder. It is the translation of the Greek word επισκοπος (*episcopos*), meaning *overseer*, and from which the word Episcopal is derived. Thus in Acts xx. 17 and 28, we find Paul addressing the *Elders* as the overseers or *Bishops* of the flock; not as a distinct order of ministers. They were the elders of the church of Ephesus, who both *ruled* and *taught* the people of God. Thus in our own church, under its present arrangement, there are two or more Presbyters or Elders, one of whom preaches the word, and administers the ordinances of the gospel, while the others assist him in the government and discipline of the church.

We are therefore called Presbyterian. The name has relation to our form of government, and is derived from Πρεσβυτερος (*Presbuteros*), a Greek word signifying an aged person or elder.

Our officers have equal power as such; though especial honour is given to those who labour in word and doctrine, as the ministers and pastors of the flock. They are esteemed "very highly for their *work's sake*," and not because as Bishops they have any higher authority to rule in the church. Hence, in our various courts there is always required an equal number of ministers and ruling elders from each congregation, who have an equal voice in all their deliberations and decisions, and to them the government and care of the church is committed.

Such are the prominent features of the Presbyterian system. We may well love and honour the name. It is derived from an office familiar to the Jewish worshippers. It was the title which the apostles recognized and bore. It was the name which their successors received, and was the badge of their office, and we adopt it, not because it is brought to us by a dim and uncertain tradition, but is found on the pages of the word of God, whence alone we derive our faith and our worship. And our church has ever struggled against error and sin, and battled earnestly for the truth. It has had great and noble men for its soldiers, and has enjoyed abundant tokens of God's blessing and approbation. The Holy Spirit has been largely poured upon it, and its order and doctrines have ever promoted pure religion. Where it has prevailed, there has been most of freedom, and virtue, and happiness. For this we love and prize it, and as we look upon it, in all its simplicity and beauty, we can sing with the Psalmist,

How decent, and how wise,
How glorious to behold,
Beyond the pomp that charms the eyes,
And rites adorned with gold.

CHAPTER II.

THE CHURCH VISIBLE AND INVISIBLE—OF WHOM COMPOSED.

THE word *church* is used in two important senses, in the Confession of Faith, and the distinction therein made is clearly affirmed in the Holy Scriptures.

1. It signifies the whole body of Christ's redeemed people. Thus it is said, "The catholic or universal church, which is *invisible*, consists of the whole number of the elect, that have been, are, or shall be gathered into one, under Christ, the head thereof; and is the spouse, the body, the fullness of him that filleth all in all." It is of this invisible church that it is written, Eph. v. 25, "Christ loved the church, and gave himself for it, that he might present it a glorious church, not having spot or wrinkle or any such thing." This is the most precious and important sense of the word. It will thus be understood and loved, when all sects, and parties, and denominations shall have been forgotten. This is the "whole family in heaven and earth," that is named after Christ. It is the

"general assembly and church of the first-born, whose names are written in heaven."

Many of its members are already with Christ, and see him as he is. Others are still in the world, while myriads yet remain to be gathered in from every nation and tribe. This invisible church embraces those of every name who truly love God, and bear the image of the Saviour.

They may belong to no peculiar creed; they may never have had the privileges of the sanctuary; they may be unknown to the world—yet Christ may recognize them as his disciples, and own them as such in that day when he shall make up his jewels. To become a member of this invisible church "neither circumcision availeth anything, nor uncircumcision, but a new creature."

2. The second sense in which the word *church* is used, refers to those who *profess* the Christian religion. Thus, in the Confession of Faith, we read, "The *visible* church, which is also catholic, or universal, under the gospel (not confined to one nation as before under the law,) consists of all those throughout the world who profess the true religion, together with their children, and is the kingdom of our Lord Jesus Christ, and the family of God, out of which there is no ordinary possibility of salvation."

The word "*catholic*," which is here used, is explained as meaning *universal*, (not the Romish church,) but all who profess the gospel of Christ, and the doctrines which are therein contained.

It includes, therefore, all the various denominations, who, while differing from each other in many particulars, receive the word of God as their only rule of faith and practice, and observe the ordinances commanded by our Lord Jesus Christ. It is called visible because its members are known, and are distinguishable from the world by their profession. Its ceremonies and its appointments fall under the observation of men like those of any other society.

On the contrary, the invisible church cannot thus be discovered. The qualifications for admission thereto are formed, and can only certainly be discerned, in the heart. It is possible for a man to be a member of the one church, while he has no connection with the other. Judas was a professed disciple of Christ, and belonged to the visible church, yet perished; while the dying thief, without the enjoyment of any outward rite, was acknowledged as a member of the invisible church, and went to Paradise. The relation of these two departments of the kingdom of Christ to each other, is that of the scaffolding to the building

It does not constitute it, yet is essential to its completion. It is the means by which sinners are converted, Christians edified and comforted, and souls saved.

When the topstone is laid, and the last redeemed sinner brought home to glory, there will be no longer need of a ministry, and ordinances, and means of grace, but together, in the temple not made with hands, all the ransomed of the Lord will be kings and priests unto God, and will serve him day and night for ever.

The visible church is said to "consist of all those throughout the world that *profess the true religion, together with their children.*" The word of God abundantly confirms the truth of this description. The promise of Christ, "where two or three are gathered together in my name, there am I in the midst of them," forms a church wherever there is a Bible, and a people who love and worship God. An open profession or avowal of faith in Christ constitutes man a member of his visible church. So that, from Adam to Abraham, all who received the promises of a coming Redeemer, and who worshipped in the faith of them, constituted the visible kingdom of Christ. But when the Lord called Abraham, and set him and his family apart as a distinct and separate people, he covenanted to be a God to him, and his seed after him, (Gen. xvii. 7,) and gave to him the rite of circumcision, which was to be the sign of admission to the visible church, and to be administered to the children, as well as to the parents. Not only Isaac, from whom the Jews were to descend, but Ishmael, and the servants of Abraham, were circumcised. So that this was evidently intended to include all of Abraham's *family*, as sharing in the covenant with him, and to be blessed for his sake.

But the promise, made to Abraham, was meant for all who in every age should fear God.

In Gal. iii. 8, it is written, "The Scriptures, foreseeing that God would justify the heathen through faith, preached before the gospel unto Abraham, saying, In thee shall all nations be blessed." These promises were of spiritual blessings, and they were made to both the believer and his children, "Abraham and his seed." Four hundred and thirty years after this covenant was made, it was renewed with the people at Sinai, having still the same provisions. For Paul declares, "The covenant which was confirmed before of God in Christ, the law which was four hundred and thirty years after, cannot disannul that it should make the promise of none effect." This promise was the object of pleasing contemplation to the saints in all ages. The Psalmist declared, "The mercy of the Lord is from everlasting to ever lasting unto such as fear him, and his righteousness unto children's children. Nor was this promise ever withdrawn. Jesus Christ took the children in his arms, and said, "Of such is the kingdom of heaven," "Suffer them to come unto me." When the apostles met the multitude, on the day of Pentecost, they urged them to repent and be baptized, adding as the reason, "for the promise is to you and to your children." Thus far not a word is said that leads us to suppose, that in the church under the Christian dispensation, any change was made respecting its members. A converted Jew who had always regarded his children as belonging to the church, was nowhere told that under Christ they were to be excluded.

And the apostle Paul taught that the Christian church was founded on the old promises to Abraham. He compares the Jewish church in his Epistle to the Romans to the good olive tree, into which, under the new dispensation, the Gentile church is grafted. In the Epistle to the Galatians, he calls all who believe "Abraham's seed and heirs, according to the promise." But what is that promise? It is to be a God to him and his seed after him.

The church therefore now, as in the days of the Patriarch, consists of all who profess the true religion, with their children. And the propriety of this divine arrangement is apparent, in the object for which the church was organized. It was established as the means of introducing souls to the blessings of salvation, and to the spiritual and invisible kingdom of Jesus Christ, to which it was subordinate. The intimate relation of parents to their children was introduced by an all-wise God, as one of the most important influences by which the great end of the church could be attained. Hence, in the covenant which Jehovah made with his professing people, he included their children in the promised blessings. And though the seals of that covenant have been changed, it is still true that the "seed of the faithful have no less a right to them now, than the children of Abraham under a former dispensation." God has never blotted out their names from his covenant, nor reversed that promise which is the enduring platform of the visible church; "I will establish my covenant between me and thee, and thy seed after thee in their generations for an everlasting covenant; to be a God to thee and thy seed after thee."

CHAPTER III.

THE OFFICERS AND DISCIPLINE OF THE CI JRCH.

THE form of government which, since the Reformation, has given the name of "Presbyterian" to one branch of the visible church is of very early origin. Long before the coming of Christ, and even before the establishment of the ceremonial law, we are told of the Elders of Israel, (Ex. iii. 16,) to whom were evidently committed the inspection and government of the people, and the settlement of all disputes among them. In Exodus xviii., we read that Moses chose wise and able men out of the tribes, whom he made rulers, and who are elsewhere called *Elders.*

The arrangement, afterwards made, of the tabernacle and temple services, was designed to set forth, in types and symbols, the office and work of the coming Messiah. Hence, priests, and sacrafices, and offerings were appointed, which were to be the "shadow of good things to come," and to cease when Christ should have appeared, as the High Priest of his people, offering "himself a sacrifice once for all."

Nor even while the temple remained was it possible for all the people to meet there for their ordinary religious services. Hence, synagogues were established, which, though divested of all the splendour of the temple, were yet convenient and proper places for prayer and praise. Here the people met to worship. Here the law was read and expounded, and the promises of God made the theme of devout and grateful contemplation.

The officers of the synagogue were Elders, or Presbyters. One of them presided over the assembly, and was called the "ruler of the synagogue," as in Mark v. 22, Luke viii. 41, and Acts xiii. 15. The others were his counsellors, who took part in the government of the congregation, and to whom all cases of discipline were committed. See John xii. 42; 2 Cor. xi. 24.

Besides these officers there were Deacons, who collected the alms of the people and distributed to the poor. There was also a high court of appeal, called the Great Synagogue, where errors in the lower courts might be corrected. This was the general system of church government throughout the nation. It was a system of representation familiar to all the Jews, and by which they were bound together as one body, though having many members.

When Christ appeared he recognized and approved the worship and government of the synagogue, as was evident by his frequent presence there, while his apostles, following his example, often met the people and instructed them in these popular assemblages of the Jews.

To the early disciples, therefore, the form of government which we now call presbyterial was familiar, and it is easy to see how readily the Christian church might adopt it. And that this was the form which it assumed, is evident from the fact that its officers have the names and duties which formerly belonged to the officers of the synagogue. We no where meet among them the names of the *Priesthood;* but we are continually told of "*Elders* being ordained in every church;" and of the "*Elders* of the church being called together;" and of the "*Elders* that rule well, and labour in word and doctrine."

Hence, while the apostles could not, in the nature of their duties as such, appoint successors to the apostolic office, as *Ministers* and *Elders* they "set apart faithful men, who should be able to TEACH others also."

It was by "laying on of the hands of the *Presbytery*" that Timothy received the gift of the ministry. And when the apostles gave advice and counsel, it was as *Elders*, speaking to fellow Presbyters. Thus the apostle Peter writes (1 Peter, v. 1): "The Elders which are among you I exhort, who *am also an Elder.*"

The Elders of the church were to be called to visit and pray over the sick. James v. 14. They were assembled to consider questions of discipline, and when any subject of interest to the church at large was to be decided, we read of a meeting of Ministers, or Apostles and Elders, at Jerusalem, whence decrees were sent to all the churches. Acts xv. 4—22.

Here we meet the general outlines of our church:

1. An equality among the Ministry.

2. The government of particular congregations by two or more Elders.

3. The union of many churches, under a council of Ministers and Elders, deciding questions of doctrine and practice.

The office of Deacon was afterwards introduced, to relieve the ministry from the care of the poor. The account of its institution, with the reasons for it, is given in Acts vi. 1—6. Some of the men thus appointed afterwards preached—not in the capacity of Deacons, but as Evangelists, to which office they were specially set apart. Acts xxi. 8. During the first century the church continued to be governed after the simple model of the Jewish synagogue.

Three or four men of piety and wisdom ruled in each congregation. But as the churches increased, and the duties of the ministry became more arduous, one man of superior wisdom was chosen from among the Presbyters to preside over them, who was called the angel of the church (Rev. ii. 3,) and also Bishop, or overseer. He had the care of one Christian congregation, teaching and administering the ordinances, but having no power above his fellow Elders. This was the essential plan of our own church, at the present day, and of the synagogue before and at the coming of Christ. Each particular congregation was under the care of a Presbytery of Elders, of whom one at least taught the people, while the rest assisted in the care and discipline of the church.

It is evident, in the history of the apostolic church, that the congregations were not wholly isolated and independent, but that there was a bond of union, through their ministers and representatives, which all recognized, and under which all acted. This was not a single individual, of special and superior powers, but a body of men of equal authority, whose decisions were received by the whole church. The fifteenth chapter of Acts contains a history of a council of Ministers, acting with authority on questions of vast importance to the entire Christian community, and clearly illustrating the dependence of one part of the church upon all the rest. An earnest dispute had arisen upon the subject of circumcision, between two of the apostles and certain teachers who sought to introduce a Jewish rite into the Christian church. To settle the question, delegates were sent to Jerusalem, who there met the Apostles and Elders, who considered the matter, and decided to send some of the representatives to Antioch with the decrees of the Synod, and with the assurances of their friendly interest and care for them.

Here was an ecclesiastical court, possessing not merely advisory powers, but authority to send forth decrees, which the churches were to register and keep.

Nor, when men were to be set apart to the ministerial office, did a single individual, clothed with prelatical power, perform the duty, but a company of Presbyters. It was the solemn injunction of Paul to Timothy (1 Tim. iv. 14): "Neglect not the gift that is in thee, which was given thee by prophecy, with the laying on of the hands of the Presbytery." It was by a number of Elders, consulting and praying together, that the solemn act was accomplished, which set apart the youthful Timothy to the work of the holy ministry. We no where in the New Testament meet with any facts which show that the work of discipline and of ordination was performed in any other way than by a union of two or more co-Presbyters, of equal power and authority, acting together. Here are all the prominent features of the Presbyterian church, as already stated.

But in the course of years, as the churches (first and naturally established in the cities) began to form and assist congregations in the smaller and less important places, their pastors continued their inspection and care over them, sending out deputies, or assistant ministers, to preach among them. These assistants were called "chorepiscopoi," or "country bishops," and assumed a middle rank between Bishops and Elders. It was not long before the city pastors, who were chosen to preside in their presbyterial meetings, assumed new powers and authority, claiming supremacy over the churches in certain districts, (afterwards called dioceses,) and superiority to their Ministers or Presbyters. It was this departure from the simplicity of the gospel, and from the *positive rule* of Christ, which forbade any strife for pre-eminence, that in the course of a few centuries made the church corrupt, filled it with a ministry destitute of the Spirit of Christ, and that changed the simple ordinances of the gospel into a round of rites and ceremonies, borrowed from the temple service and from the worship of heathen idolaters.

Then, as was foretold, the true church fled into the wilderness from before her enemies, and there, among the mountains, nourished and kept alive the truth and worship of God, while the whole world went after the lying wonders of the mother of abominations.

CHAPTER IV.

THE WORSHIP AND ORDINANCES OF THE CHURCH.

As the government of the Christian church was arranged after the model of the Jewish synagogue, its *worship* also partook of the same simple and pure character. The evident tendency of the gospel was to draw away the mind from any attachment to rites and forms, as essential to true religion. It taught men to regard a change of heart and a holy life, as of far more importance than any adherence to ceremonies and external modes of worship. Hence, the apostles took occasion to rebuke, most plainly, the tendency of some professing Christians to introduce the Jewish ritual into the services of the Christian church.

The first day of the week was universally set apart for the public worship of God. On that day Christ, the Lord of the Sabbath, arose from the dead, and the following passages show that it was henceforth observed as the day of rest: Mark xvi. 9; John xx. 19; Matt. xxviii. 1, 8, 9; Acts xx. 7; 1 Cor. xvi. 2; Rev. i. 10. Compare also

Psalm cxviii. 24 with the foregoing. From these texts of Scripture it is evident that the apostles, with the Divine approbation and appointment, changed the day of worship from the seventh to the first day of the week.

Then the disciples gathered together, first at private houses, and afterward, as their numbers increased, in places where they were better accommodated, and over which they had more entire control. In their assemblies the principal services consisted in reading and expounding the Scriptures, exhortations, prayers, and the singing of hymns, Acts xiii. 15, 16, and xviii. 4; Heb. x. 25, and xiii. 15; Matt. xxvi. 30. Christ himself appointed two ordinances only—Baptism and the Lord's Supper.

BAPTISM was the rite of initiation into the church. It was an application of water to the body, in token of the cleansing blood of Christ, and the renewing influences of the Holy Spirit.

Hitherto, circumcision had been the seal of the covenant, and the sign of introduction to the church. But when Christ sent forth his ministers, his command was to teach and to *baptize* the nations. This was only changing the seals but not the covenant. Hence the apostles, rehearsing the promises to believers and their children, baptized them and their families. Thus when the jailor believed, they baptized him and "all his." Acts xvi. 33. When Lydia was converted, she and her household were baptized, Acts xvi. 15. Paul speaks (1 Cor. i. 16,) of baptizing "the household of Stephanas."

The mode of baptism is not essential to the validity of the ordinance. It is a token of purification, and may be accomplished by pouring or sprinkling, or by immersion. The word which is translated "*baptize*," has various significations, and we are not necessarily confined to any one of them. It implies to wash, to tinge, to dye with any liquid, to sprinkle, to dip. Many passages in the word of God occur in which the word must necessarily signify to pour upon, or to sprinkle.

The ceremonial washing (baptism) of cups, and pots, and brazen vessels, and tables, was by sprinkling, not immersion. The promise of Christ that his disciples should be *baptized* with the Holy Ghost, was fulfilled by the *pouring* of the Spirit upon them. The prophecy of John, "that Christ should baptize with fire," was accomplished at the time when cloven tongues of fire sat upon each of the disciples.

Baptism is admitted by all to signify the cleansing and renovation of the soul by the Spirit. In the promises to the church respecting that Spirit, he is spoken of as being poured out. Isaiah xxxii. 15, and xliv. 3. In Ezekiel xxxvi. 25, we read, "I will sprinkle clean water upon you, and ye shall be clean."

Isaiah says of Christ, "So shall he *sprinkle* many nations." And the apostle speaks of the "blood of *sprinkling*." The blood of the paschal lamb was *sprinkled* upon the door posts of the houses of the Israelites, a fit emblem of that blood by which we are cleansed.

Thus the language of Scripture points out to us sprinkling as the most appropriate manner of baptism, and as significant of the work of the Spirit.

The *circumstances* under which many were baptized, also show that this mode must have been in common use with the apostles. Three thousand were baptized in a part of a day, in a populous city, and at a time when the streams near it were dry.

Ananias went into the house where Saul was, after he had been met in his way to Damascus, and said, "Arise and be baptized;" and when he had received sight, he arose and forthwith was baptized, and then ate and was strengthened.

Cornelius was converted under the preaching of Peter, and when the Holy Ghost fell upon him and his company, the apostle asked, "Can any man forbid water that these should not be baptized?"

The jailor was converted at midnight, and the same hour was baptized. All these scenes evidently occurred in *the house*, where the only mode in which water could be applied, was by sprinkling or pouring. The history of the church, after the times of the apostles, shows that then, as now, baptism was administered either by plunging the body in water, or by sprinkling, and that either mode was considered a proper compliance with the command of Christ.

The Scriptures seek to guard us against any such attachment to a particular manner of administering Christian ordinances, as shall draw our minds away from the thing signified. What we need is the renewing influences of the Spirit; if we are thus cleansed, a drop of water as well as an ocean, can signify to our hearts the "blood of sprinkling, which speaketh better things than that of Abel." If we have not this change,

> "Nor running brook, nor flood, nor sea
> Can wash our dismal stains away."

Besides the ordinance of baptism, or the rite of introduction to the church, our Saviour instituted the *Lord's Supper*, which he designed to be a part of the worship of his people. On the evening before he was crucified, he and his disciples were gathered in an upper chamber, at Jerusalem, to eat the Passover, commemorative of the deliverance of Israel from the bondage of Egypt. While they were still at the table, Jesus took bread and blessed it, and gave it to his disciples to eat as a memorial of his body broken for sin. In the same manner also he took the cup, and when he had given thanks, bade them all drink of it, as a memorial of his blood which was shed for the remission of sins. The apostle Paul, when he was writing to the churches in relation to the design of this ordinance, declared, "As oft as ye eat this bread and drink this cup, ye do show forth the Lord's death until he come." When, therefore, Christians celebrate the Lord's Supper, they testify before the world to their belief in Christ, and their confidence that he was crucified for their sins. This ordinance is called sometimes "the communion," because in it we hold fellowship with Christ and his people. 1 Cor. x. 16, 17. When properly received, it serves to strengthen our faith and quicken our graces, and leads us to cherish a warmer love for Him who hath spread the feast, and bids us as guests to partake of it. This was evidently the design of Christ in establishing this sacrament, that it should serve as a memorial of him, and its value was to be in proportion to the degree of *faith* and love in which it should be received He established no rite which of itself secured the salvation of the soul. *He alone* is the way, and the truth, and the life, and the ordinances of his house are only means of grace designed to lead the soul to him. They are only valuable when they produce this result. This our church teaches, when it declares in the Confession of Faith, "That the grace which is exhibited in, or by the sacraments, rightly used, is not conferred by any power in them; neither doth the efficacy of a sacrament depend upon the piety, or intention of him that doth administer it, but upon the work of the Spirit, and the word of institution, which contains, together with a precept authorizing the use thereof, a promise of benefit to worthy receivers."

Such are the ordinances of the church as established by Christ and the apostles. They were the simple rites of the early Christians, before they were distorted and perverted by the pompous and unmeaning ceremonies of a corrupt church, and are received by us as the form of worship best adapted to lead the mind upward to God, who as a Spirit requires us to worship him in spirit and in truth.

CHAPTER V.

CORRUPTIONS OF THE CHURCH.

THE simplicity and purity of the primitive church, in its worship and government, was retained throughout the age of the apostles and their immediate successors. The testimony of the early fathers clearly shows that the cardinal features of the Presbyterian church, viz., the parity of the ministry—the government of each separate congregation by a board of elders, teaching and ruling; and the union of all the churches under a common bond of responsibility and authority, composed of a proper representation, were the essential elements of the apostolic and primitive church.

But it was clearly foretold by the writers both of the Old and New Testament, that a great corruption and heresy should arise in the church, which should greatly mar its peace and purity, and wholly change its rites and ordinances from their original nature and intention.

More than five centuries before the coming of

Christ, the prophet Daniel predicted tne rise and progress of a religious power that should "speak great words against the Most High, and should wear out the saints of the Most High, and think to change times and laws." Dan. vii. 8—25. After the establishment of the Christian church the apostles Paul and John most distinctly warned their brethren of the coming of antichrist, and described all its principal features, its alarming progress, and its dreadful end, when Christ should destroy it with the brightness of his coming.

In 2 Thess. ii. 3—10, and 1 Tim. iv. 1—3, the power is plainly alluded to as the "son of perdition"—"the man of sin"—"the mystery of iniquity"—"the wicked whose coming is after the working of Satan with all power, and signs, and lying wonders"—"forbidding to marry, commanding to abstain from meats"—"speaking lies in hypocrisy." To the beloved disciple, amid the sublime visions of Patmos, the same spiritual power was revealed as soon to rise and corrupt the church and the world.

The wonderful descriptions given in Rev. xiii. 11—18, and xvii. 1—18, can only find their realization in the long and dark history of that church which is "drunk with the blood of the saints." Scarcely had the last apostle left the world, when this evil began to manifest itself.

It was first apparent in the ambition and pride of the pastors of the church. By the means of councils, which began in the second century to claim authority as to faith and practice, the equality of the Presbyters was at length destroyed. The Bishops of certain cities claimed a superiority over their brethren, and gradually introduced different orders of the ministry.

To support these claims, it was asserted that the officers of the Christian church were the successors to the various orders of the Jewish priesthood; that the Bishop took the place of the high-priest under the Mosaic law; and that the Presbyters and Deacons answered to the offices of priests and Levites under the same dispensation.

In order also to remove the objections which were made to the Christian faith by Jews and heathen, that its worship was so simple, many ceremonies and rites were introduced which Christ had never authorized.

Ministers began to wear robes in their services in imitation of the Jewish priests, and to use certain symbols, borrowed from the heathen, to teach the truths of religion. Thus the sign of the cross was used in baptism, and all the ordinances of religion became burdened with a weight of pompous and unmeaning ceremonies that wholly concealed the beauty and simplicity of the gospel.

As the power of the Bishops increased, they assumed more and more of the pomp and splendour which was witnessed in the Roman court. They had their thrones, and their splendid vestments, and their symbols of authority. Then were built costly and magnificent churches, enriched with gold and silver vessels for the services of religion, and adorned with paintings and images. The rich were encouraged to erect houses of worship, by being permitted to appoint the ministers who should officiate in them.

After the persecutions which raged during the first three centuries had ceased, the government and worship of the church rapidly lost all its original features. When Constantine, the emperor of Rome, exerted his power to protect the Christian religion, the church and the state were united, and ambitious and ungodly men soon began to make the office of the ministry the means of securing their own selfish purposes. Imitating the government of the empire, which was divided into provinces, (each under the care of a prefect,) the church was divided into four dioceses, over which a Bishop was appointed, who was afterwards called the Patriarch, and who had the pre-eminence over all the pastors in their district. These prelates had their seats at Rome, Antioch, Alexandria, and

Constantinople, from which cities their patriarchates were named. They had at first equal power, but gradually the Bishop of Rome usurped authority, until, in the year 606, Boniface obtained the title of universal Bishop or Pope, and was made supreme head of the church. Here was a bold, daring act of treason against Christ, who is the only Head of the church, and who has never appointed any one to fill his place. In the next century the Pope was made a temporal prince by Pepin, a French monarch. Since that time, as was predicted, he has had great power, and kings and nations have submitted to his authority. Such was the rise of the "Man of Sin." And thus did a large portion of the visible church fall away after his "lying wonders."

The church lost its original features, and became the arena where a corrupt and ambitious priesthood strove for honours and distinctions which Christ never warranted, and which the apostles never established.

The change which took place in the church, by the destruction of the equality of the ministry, was but the index of a more fearful change that the morals and doctrines of the professed disciples of Christ were undergoing. Superstition gradually took the place of true piety. The churches dedicated professedly to Him who requires spiritual worship, began to rival the ancient temple at Jerusalem, in the vestments of their priests, and the gorgeous services which they performed. Clouds of incense arose before the images which were, at the close of the fourth century, introduced for the worship of the church. The memory of the martyrs was kept alive by festivals in honour of them; rites and bombastic prayers and liturgies were multiplied; the Lord's Supper was celebrated with unnecessary frequency, and often at the tombs of martyrs, and at funerals. Imitating the tricks of heathen priests, rumors were artfully circulated of miracles performed in certain places, by which crowds were drawn thither, and the wealth and the power of the church augmented. Then an undue value was attached to a mortification of the body; and fasts were multiplied, and made essential parts of the worship of the church, and men began to shut themselves up in places of seclusion, turning away from all the duties and pleasures of life, to the cells and cloisters of hermits and monks. Even marriage was at length forbidden to ministers, and one of God's own institutions was thus disregarded and set at nought. Rapidly, now, did all traces of the gospel as first preached, and of the church as first established, disappear. The ordinance of baptism, from being a simple sign and seal, was looked upon as of itself securing pardon for sin. The Lord's Supper was changed from its original intention, as an ordinance commemorative of Christ's death, to an actual sacrifice, and the bread and wine were set forth as the real body and blood of the dying Saviour. Hence arose the custom of receiving the sacrament while kneeling, instead of the usual posture of guests, as it was first received by the disciples.

Then, as the idea of sacerdotal power and authority advanced, the people were taught to confess their sins in private to their ministers, who now assumed the name and offices of priests, instead of being simply "ambassadors for Christ, to beseech men to be reconciled to God."

Such was the progress of corruption in the church, and the growth of that "mystery of iniquity" clearly foretold by the prophets and apostles. No prophecy was more distinctly fulfilled than that found in the Epistles of Paul and John. No power has been a more potent engine of evil than that which had now arisen.

Gradually did it increase, until all nations were subject thereto. Learning was diminished, and the state of the church became fearfully dark and corrupt. The popes were monsters of wickedness, the offices of the church were bought and sold, and all the institutions of religion were made a means of increasing the wealth of the proud and ambitious men who appeared as the pretended teachers of the gospel of the meek and lowly Jesus. Pardon for past sins, and indulgences to commit new ones, were sold for money. Prisons and tortures, and death in its most horrid forms, became the arguments by which the bloody and rapacious priesthood maintained their authority and confirmed their doctrines. Men of the most abandoned character were elevated to be the pretended successors of St. Peter, and the lives of the priests and prelates were for ages blackened by every form of vice. They who affirm that salvation depends on receiving the rites of religion from ministers ordained by such power, must trace their authority through these corruptions.

The midnight of darkness and ignorance now rested, like a pall of death, upon the nations, and the wondrous revelations of the holy prophets were fully confirmed.

Babylon the great has become "the habitation of devils, and the hold of every foul spirit, and a cage of every unclean and hateful bird," and "her sins have reached unto heaven."

The following table will place before the eye a succinct view of the rise and progress of the Papal corruptions, together with the chief events that marked the history of the church of Christ up to the Reformation.

CHRONOLOGICAL TABLE OF THE CHURCH.

1st Century.	*The church modeled after the Jewish Synagogue.*—Each assembly governed by a bench of Ruling and Teaching Elders. Deacons. Baptism and the Lord's Supper instituted. Parity of the clergy.	1st and 2d persecutions of Christians.
2d Century.	Bishop's authority augmented by Councils.—The idea of succession to the Jewish hierarchy arose. Ceremonies multiplied.—god-fathers and god-mothers in Baptism.	3d and 4th persecutions.
3d Century.	Bishops of cities assume new powers. Monastic life came in fashion. Churches first erected.—Sacraments corrupted.—Sign of the Cross used. Incense first offered. Fasting common. Oblations for the dead.	5th, 6th, 7th, and 8th persecutions. Novatians. Witnesses for the truth.
4th Century.	Diocesan Episcopacy. Archbishops. Magnificent churches erected.—Rights of patronage. Parts of public worship changed. Celibacy of the clergy. *Pious frauds. Image worship.* Pretended discovery of the true cross. Pilgrimages in repute. *Relics* esteemed. Word Mass adopted. Wax candles kept burning in churches. Canonical hours for prayer.	9th and 10th persecutions. Christianity tolerated. Versions of the Scriptures.

Century		
5th Century.	*Patriarchs having power over bishops.* The bishop of Rome augmenting his power. Clergy licentious and worldly. Monks becoming opulent and influential. *Pictures and images introduced.* Prayers for the dead. Lights used in churches during day. Feasts of Advent and Palm Sunday, and the superstition of Ash-Wednesday, commenced about 430.—Private confession introduced.	Nestorius condemned for refusing to call Mary "the mother of God." *St. Patrick.*
6th Century.	*Cardinal Bishops of Rome.* Clergy corrupt. Increase of superstition. Temples in honour of Saints erected. *Canon of the Mass,* by which the Lord's Supper was esteemed a sacrifice. Extreme Unction. Holy Water. Image worship suppressed. Benedictine Monks.	Nestorians spreading the gospel in the East. *Columba. Iona.*
7th Century.	Pope Boniface III. made Universal Bishop by the Emperor Phocas, A. D. 606. *Mahomet* 612. Learning low. Bishops ignorant.—Churches made a protection to all who fled to them. Rites multiplied. Monastic institutions increased. Feast in honour of the true cross.	Culdees.

8th CENTURY.	*Pope of Rome made a temporal prince by Pepin.* Bishops venerated by the people and invested with regal domains. Riches of the church increase. Kissing the Pope's foot. Image worship restored. People first buried in church-yards and consecrated ground. Feasts multiplied.	Church in the wilderness. Christians in the valleys of Piedmont.
9t. CENTURY.	DARK AGES. TRANSUBSTANTIATION. Rites multiplied. Veneration for saints and relics. Pope Boniface expelled from his office on account of his abominable wickedness. Pope Stephen, a still more outrageous monster than Boniface, seized, and strangled in his prison.	Claude of Turin. Paulicians and Waldenses
10th CENTURY.	*Popes are monsters.* This age called the Iron for its barbarity and the Dark Age for its ignorance. *Agnus Dei invented.* Pope John deposed, for drinking the Devil's health, and for other most nefarious practices. Pope Leo caught in adultery, and slain by the husband. Consecration of Bells introduced. Cursing by bell, book, and candle-light invented. A boy five years old made prelate of Rheims.	Waldenses witnesses for the truth.

11th Century.	*Crusades.* Popo Benedict banished from tho popedom for his wickedness. Silvester also expelled. Gregory VI. elected. They all reside in Rome among their respective votaries. A Council at Sutrium expelled them all, and Clement II. elected. Thus four Popes were living at the same time. *Beads to pray by first introduced.* Order of Flagellantes.	Paulicians numerous.
12th Century.	The number of Sacraments fixed at seven. Indulgences to commit crime.	Noble Lesson.
13th Century.	Cardinals first wore Red Hats. Crusade against the Albigenses : nearly 100,000 put to death by Papists.—Auricular Confession instituted. The Inquisition eslished.	Bible divided into chapters.
14th Century.	Indulgences *first publicly sold.* Seat of the Popes removed from Rome to Avignon.	*Wickliffe.*
15th Century.	John Huss, a Christian martyr, burned at Constance, in violation of the Emperor's safeguard, and in conformity to the decree of the ungodly council, that "No faith is to be kept with heretics." *Inquisition* established in Castile.	Huss and Jerome of Prague *Vulgate Bible.*
16th Century.	Institution of Jesuits. Massacre of Waldenses and of St. Bartholomew.	Reformation.

CHAPTER VI.

WITNESSES FOR THE TRUTH—THE WALDENSES.

THE sombre shadows of the picture at which we have glanced, are relieved by one long line of light, which gathered brightness amid the deepening gloom of Papal darkness and corruption. During the dreadful defection of God's ancient people, when the prophet Elijah was heard complaining, amid the solitudes of Horeb, "I alone am left," it was the declaration of Him who knew the hearts of men, "Yet I have left me seven thousand in Israel, all the knees which have not bowed unto Baal, and every mouth which hath not kissed him." So, also, when the visible church was losing its purity, and its lineaments were fading into the dark and distorted features of the mystery of iniquities, were there men of pure lives and simple faith, who remained steadfast, and kept alive the knowledge of the truth and the spiritual worship of God. This was the subject of distinct notice by the same prophecies that described the rise and progress of the Papacy and its corruptions.

In the eleventh and twelfth chapters of Revelations, undoubted allusions are made to the history and perpetuity of the church, amidst all the fearful assaults of her enemies. It is there revealed, under the symbol of a woman fleeing before the great red dragon, that the disciples of Christ should retire from their persecutors, and find peace and safety amid the solitudes of the wilderness.

Describing this wondrous history, yet seen by the apostle only in the future, it is written:

"And when the dragon saw that he was cast unto the earth, he persecuted the woman which brought forth the man-child.

"And to the woman were given two wings of a great eagle, that she might fly into the wilderness, into her place; where she is nourished for a time, and times, and half a time, from the face of the serpent.

"And the serpent cast out of his mouth water as a flood, after the woman, that he might cause her to be carried away of the flood.

"And the earth helped the woman; and the earth opened her mouth, and swallowed up the flood which the dragon cast out of his mouth.

"And the dragon was wroth with the woman,

and went to make war with the remnant of her seed, which keep the commandments of God, and have the testimony of Jesus Christ."

With what minuteness this has been fulfilled the history of the church abundantly testifies. The people of God when persecuted in one city fled to another, and at length found safety and a home amid the fastnesses of the mountains. Nor has there ever been a link wanting in the chain of witnesses who have, from the age of the apostles to the present hour, borne testimony to the blessed truths of the gospel.

The Christian church was first organized at Jerusalem. What were its general features we have already seen. Formed of converts from the Jewish faith, it evidently assumed that model to which they had long been familiar, and which, in its simplicity of detail, and its republican character and tendency, has ever been connected with, and the firm supporter of, truth and liberty.

When persecution at length scattered the church at Jerusalem, the disciples went everywhere preaching the gospel, until the knowledge of Jesus Christ was carried throughout the known world.

In this work the apostle Paul bore a conspicuous part, as the great missionary to the Gentiles. He visited Italy; and tradition affirms, fulfilled his desire expressed in Romans xv. 24—28, and preached the gospel in Spain. It is also said that his way thither was by the Cottian Alps, over which a high road was built for the use of the Roman legions, traces of which still exist. The history of the New Testament teaches us that to him, and not to Peter, as the Papal traditions affirm, was Italy indebted for the establishment of the church. He it was who wrote out for the Romans that wonderful epitome of the gospel called after their name. He it was who, dwelling in Rome a prisoner, though in his own hired house, met his brethren there, and explained to them the principles of that rising sect "every where spoken against." Paul, and not Peter, was the founder of the Italian church, as is evident from the record found in the Acts of the Apostles. When he passed away to his reward, the truths he revealed were still working out their blessed results, and making their way among the inhabitants of Italy. But the storms of persecution were beginning to try the faith of the people of God, and at length Christianity, banished from the courts of monarchs and the abodes of luxury, sought and found a peaceful home amid the valleys of the Alps.

At the foot of those lofty mountains, which form the rugged boundary of Italy, France, and

Switzerland, nestle the smiling valleys of Piedmont. Far above them rise, in stern grandeur, the hoary monuments of the Creator's power, placed there like watchful sentinels, to guard the repose of the simple-hearted people whose homes they shelter. Wild and narrow defiles—foaming torrents, rushing down their mountain bed, and wearing a course among the rocks to the streams below—peaceful lakes, embosomed in the hills, and reflecting like polished mirrors the rugged outlines of nature—glaciers, that sparkle in the sunlight—mountains, covered with eternal snow—and meadows of unrivalled beauty and fertility, form a contrast of awful grandeur, and attractive grace and loveliness. This is the home of the WALDENSES. Here Christianity fled, when the persecutions of the second and third centuries were confirming the apocalyptic vision of the woman fleeing into the wilderness, from the dragon who sought to destroy her and her child.

Here, from the early ages of the church, has been the abode of a pure and primitive Christianity, where the truth has been held as it was first delivered to the saints, and the worship of God and the order of his house have been unsullied by the admixture of human tradition and senseless mummeries. Romish historians have indeed denied this, and affirm that the Waldenses originated in the twelfth century; and a few Protestant writers have fallen into the same error, supposing that this people owe their origin to Waldo, a merchant of Lyons, who attempted a reformation in the church. But the researches of many distinguished men have shown, that by well authenticated tradition the Vaudois church has existed where it now has its home, from the times of the early persecutions, if not from the apostles themselves. They formed a part of the visible church before those corruptions which crept into it had introduced the Man of Sin, and the mystery of iniquity. They did not separate from the church of Rome, but they who introduced Catholicism gradually separated from them, by those modifications of the worship of the early church, and corruptions of its order and faith, which have already been noticed.

Amid the wealth and splendour of the cities, those who professed Christianity manifested a constant tendency to suit their ceremonies and rites to the tastes of the people, long familiarized to the pomp and splendour of courts, and to the gorgeous displays of heathen worship. Hence arose the Catholic church. But these temptations were unfelt amid those secluded valleys which sheltered the simple-hearted Vaudois.

Amongst them, therefore, the pure and spiritual worship and doctrines which were preached by the first disciples of the Christian faith, were handed down unimpaired from generation to generation. In the long and bitter persecutions to which this people have been subject, many of their ancient records perished in the flames. Yet authentic portions of their history have been preserved, and even the testimony of their enemies has, by an overruling Providence, been made to establish the proof that they have been the conservators of a pure Christianity, while the whole world was going after the lying wonders of a false religion.

Reinerius, who wrote bitterly against them, declares "that among all the sects which are, or ever were, none have been more pernicious to Rome than that of the Leonists (or Waldenses);" and among other causes, he gives this as the first, "*that it is the most ancient of all*, since some affirm that it has continued from the time of Sylvester, or from the times of the apostles."

In the library of the University of Geneva is an ancient manuscript, dated in the year 1100 (60 years before Waldo is mentioned,) which speaks of the Vaudois; and another history, of nearly the same age, contains several sermons from the Waldensian pastors, and a treatise on

Antichrist. It is among these inhabitants of the valleys that we find the church of Christ during the long night of Papal darkness; and here were preserved those principles and doctrines which are now received and taught as the distinctive features of the gospel. (See Note A.)

The Waldensian church is distinctly and purely Presbyterian. Its doctrines, its discipline, and its government are like those which the Presbyterian church in Scotland, Geneva and America maintains. Its officers are Bishops, Elders and Deacons, and its courts are Consistories, or Sessions, Presbyteries and Synods. At the time of the Reformation it extended its sympathy and its fellowship to those Reformers who adopted the Presbyterian order and doctrines; and our ministers who visit them find a cordial reception and a hearty welcome. (See Note B.)

They form therefore an important link in the history of the church of Christ. Their traditions respecting their origin are, that they are descended from those followers of Christ who, escaping from the persecutions of the Roman Emperors in the second century, found a refuge in these secluded and unknown valleys. And this claim has been admitted by some of their most violent enemies, and by the most intelligent Protestant writers who have studied their history.

In the fourth century, Vigilantius, who incurred the displeasure of Rome by his opposition to its growing corruptions, retired to the Alps, and found sympathy and peace among the inhabitants of the valleys.

Early in the seventh century the Paulicians, who, under their leader Constantine, had suffered severe persecutions, and were driven from place to place by their enemies, also found a home among the Alpine hills. They became the objects of hatred to the Romish church, because of their opposition to image worship and to the hierarchy.

In the eighth century, Claude, the Bishop of Turin, attempted a reformation of the church, and was aided in his efforts by the Vaudois, whose homes were in the district assigned to him as his pastoral charge. During those ages of darkness which followed, little information of these witnesses for Christ can be gleaned, except that among them were still found those who manfully maintained the truth, against the superstitions that were rapidly gaining ground in the Papal church, and the unscriptural assumptions of the Pope of Rome. In the year 1100 was written the "Noble Lesson." This was a compendium of Waldensian doctrine, wholly repudiating the errors of the Catholic creed, and harmonizing with the faith which we now receive as once delivered to the saints. The following is the conclusion of the Lesson:

"We have only to imitate Jesus Christ, and to do his pleasure,

And to keep firmly that which he has commanded,

And to be well advised when Antichrist shall come,

That we may give no credence to his doings or sayings.

But according to Scripture there are many Antichrists,

For all who are contrary to Christ are Antichrist.

Many signs and great wonders shall be from this time forward to the day of judgment.

The heaven and the earth shall burn, and all the living shall die;

Then all shall rise again to life everlasting.

Every building shall be laid prostrate, and then shall be the last judgment, when God shall separate his people, as it is written,

Then shall he say to the wicked, Depart frcm me, ye cursed, into everlasting fire,

From which may God in his good will preserve us,

And give us to hear what he shall then say to his own people,

Come, ye blessed of my Father, inherit the kingdom prepared for you from the foundation of the world.

May it please the Lord, who formed the world, that we may be of the number of his elect to stand in his courts."

From various manuscripts which have been found among the Waldensians, it is evident that during the middle ages of Christianity that people were bearing a noble testimony to the truth, and were engaged in most earnest efforts to spread the doctrines of the cross.

From the eighth century to the fourteenth the inhabitants of the Alpine valleys were very numerous, and their missionaries went everywhere preaching Christ.

One of the objects of deepest interest at the present day among the valleys of Piedmont, is the spot where, in their theological school, their youth were trained in the knowledge of God's word, and in the duties of the holy ministry.

In the beautiful vale of Angrogna (memorable above all others for the recollections it awakens), is the Pra del Tor, a level and grassy spot of about an acre in extent, which reposes in its wild beauty amid the Alpine hills, like an oasis in the desert. The only easy access to it is through a deep gorge, in many parts of which the road is but a few feet wide. On the one side the clear waters of a mountain stream are rushing and foaming by, to mingle with those of the Pelice; while on the other, vast masses of high and overhanging rocks seem to threaten the traveller with imminent destruction. In this spot, hidden from the world, and chosen for its quiet and solitude, the Waldensian Barbes or Pastors had their "school of the prophets." And here, too, the Synod of this apostolic church often met to transact their wonted duties, and to consult respecting the interests of the kingdom of Christ. The histories of that people relate, that at some of these sessions as many as one hundred and forty ministers were convened, during the ages when their church was most prosperous, and ere it had been reduced and scattered by the horrid persecutions of the Papal priesthood. These Synods, which were then held in the valleys, were composed of the Pastors and Elders of the various parishes, meeting yearly, and making inquiry into the state of the ministers, and hearing appeals from the Consistories or Sessions of the churches.

At each Synod a President was chosen, usually called a Moderator, who had the chief authority in the Assembly, while in office, though never assuming a higher rank than his brethren, or claiming to be more than a simple minister. There is no evidence that the principles of the hierarchy were ever engrafted upon the Waldensian church. From its earliest history it has acknowledged but one form of government, and that is the Presbyterian.

Their early records show the Waldenses to have been diligent students of the word of God. Their Catholic enemies brought as a charge against them, "Whatever is preached without Scripture proof, they account no better than a fable. They hold that Holy Scripture is of the same efficacy in the vulgar tongue as in Latin. And they can say a great part of the Old Testament by heart." Another writer confesses that "the Waldenses were so well instructed in the Holy Scriptures, that he had seen peasants who could recite the whole book of Job *verbatim*, and several others who could perfectly repeat the whole of the New Testament." A monk once sent to have a conference with them, and convince them of their errors, returned in confusion, owning "that in his whole life he had never known so much of the Scriptures as he had learned during those few days that he had been conversing with the heretics." And at another time, a student of the Sorbonne, sent upon a similar errand, confessed that "he had understood more of the doctrine of salvation from the answers of the *little children*, in their catechisms, than by all the disputations which he had ever before heard." (See Note C.) Nor were they satisfied to possess the truth themselves; they desired to communicate it to others. They were imbued with the spirit of missions to an extent almost apostolic. Their missionaries went forth two by two, visiting their brethren scattered throughout Europe, and everywhere preaching Christ. It is worthy of notice, that for a period of more than six hundred years before the Reformation, the most distinguished men who attempted to introduce the light of truth upon the night of Papal error were in some way connected with the Waldenses. Such are Waldo, Peter Bruys, Henry of Lausanne, and Lollard, who in England sought to spread the doctrines of the cross. Nor did the ministers of the word alone engage in these missionary labours. Pious men, who followed the business of pedlers, would carry some leaves of the Bible, or manuscript tracts, with their packages of merchandize, or at least bear on their memories whole chapters of the Bible which they could readily repeat when opportunity presented.

The inquisitor Sacco describes these interviews in the following language. "They offer for sale to people of quality ornamental articles, such as rings and veils. After a purchase has been made, if the pedler is asked, 'Have you anything else to sell?' he answers, 'I have jewels more precious than these things; I would make you a present of them, if you would promise not to betray me to the clergy.' Having been assured on this point, he says, 'I have a pearl so brilliant, that a man by means of it may learn to know God; I have another so splendid, that it kindles the love of God in the heart of him who possesses it.' And so he brings forth the word of God, and he preaches about Christ. After his address, the heretic says to his hearer, 'Examine and consider which is the most perfect religion and the purest faith, whether ours, or that of the Romish church, and choose it, whichever it may be.' And thus being turned from the Catholic faith by such errors, he forsakes us. A person who gives credit to such discourses, who believes errors of this kind, and becomes their partizan and defender, concealing the heretic in his house for many months, is initiated in all that relates to the sect."

A people thus ardently loving the Bible, and desiring to spread the knowledge of its blessed truths, could not long escape the enmity of that apostate church which loved darkness rather than light. The "Noble Lesson" shows, that as early as the year 1100 the Vaudois were the objects of bitter hatred, because of their blameless lives and pure doctrines.

"Such an one," says the poet, "as will not curse, swear, or lie, or speak evil, or commit injustice or theft, or give himself up to dissoluteness, or take vengeance on his enemy, is called a *Waldense,* and said to be deserving of punishment; and they find occasion by lies and deceit to take from him what he has earned by fair dealing."

This enmity to the Vaudois gradually increased, until it ripened into most bitter and fearful persecution. As the Roman church, which now usurped authority over all the Christian world, began to grow darker in the night of its error and corruption, the Waldensian church seemed like a lamp to gather brightness. It was then that it began to feel the intensity of that hatred with which those who love and teach error regard the true disciples of Jesus.

In the year 1209, Otho IV. of Germany, on his visit to Rome, to be consecrated Emperor by Pope Innocent III., passed through Piedmont, and from a desire of personal revenge upon a rival gave permission to the Archbishop of Turin to destroy the Vaudois by the force of arms.

Persecution now entered those peaceful valleys, and turned them into scenes of outrage, war and blood.

The agents of the Inquisition, which had just commenced its terrible work, soon directed their brutal assaults against them. Thousands of those witnesses for the truth sealed their testimony with their blood.

The history of those dreadful scenes is unparalleled in the annals of modern persecution, and presents to us the original of that picture, drawn by inspiration, of her who, as the mystical Babylon, was seen "drunk with the blood of the saints."

The fathers of the Inquisition, at first contenting themselves with anathemas, imprisonments, and executions, at length, with all the bitter hatred which has ever characterized their accursed institution, began a general system of extermination. Early in the fifteenth century the work of death commenced, by which the inhabitants of these Alpine valleys were made to feel the cruel hand of a merciless priesthood, waging ceaseless war upon them, and exposing them to constant and terrible sufferings.

Exciting against them the most bitter hatred

among the Papists, they attacked them unexpectedly, in one of their peaceful valleys, in the early spring. Numbers were cruelly butchered. Others fled to the mountains, where many of the old and helpless perished, and fifty infants were found frozen, some in their cradles, and some clasped in their mothers' arms, who were also dead by their fearful exposure. This was the beginning of a series of persecutions, waged for centuries against the Waldenses.

From this time they were the continued objects of inquisitorial hatred, whose sufferings awakened the sympathy of the Christian world.

It was in view of their bitter sorrows that Milton, with all the deep sensibilities of his heart stirred within him, wrote these memorable lines:

"Avenge, O Lord, thy slaughtered saints, whose bones
Lie scattered on the Alpine mountains cold;
E'en them who kept thy truth so pure of old,
When all our fathers worshipped stocks and stones,
Forget not; in thy book record their groans,
Who were thy sheep; and in their ancient fold,
Slain by the bloody Piedmontese, that rolled
Mother with infant down the rocks: their moans
The vales redoubled to the hills, and they
To heaven: their martyred blood and ashes sow
O'er all the Italian fields, where still doth sway
The triple tyrant; that from these may grow
An hundred fold, who, having learnt thy way,
Early may fly the Babylonian woe."

CHAPTER VII.

THE PRIMITIVE CHURCHES OF ENGLAND, IRELAND AND SCOTLAND.

THE brief outline of Waldensian history, given in the preceding chapter, is sufficient to show that the principles and order of the Presbyterian church have been maintained in every age since the times of the apostles. That people are, to this day, the representatives of those who, early receiving the truths of the gospel, held them, in all their primitive simplicity and purity, during the long night of Papal darkness and corruption that rested upon the world.

But there were other communities which bore a noble testimony to the ancient faith during the early history of the Christian religion, and even long after the Roman prelates began to usurp authority over the consciences of men.

The early churches of England evidently embodied the essential principles of the Presbyterial order. It has been maintained by many that the gospel was introduced into Britain by the apostle Paul, and th t when he "took his journey into

Spain" he went to the islands beyond it. Whether this tradition be correct or not, it is certain that, early in the Christian era, Britain received the gospel, not from Rome, but from the churches of Asia. Before the close of the second century, many Christian communities were gathered, which in their simple faith worshipped God, wholly independent of the rising power of the Roman priesthood.

In the early part of the seventh century, when Augustine was sent from Rome to Britain, to bring that island under the Papal yoke, he found ministers and churches, which were said to have been in existence from the first century. Many of them refused to acknowledge his authority as the legate of the Pope, and chose death, rather than a renunciation of their pure faith. As late as the tenth century, at which time Prelacy had been established, Elfric, a Saxon Bishop, in announcing the orders of church officers, places the Presbyter first, adding that "there is no more difference between him and the Bishop, but that the Bishop is appointed to confer ordination—which, if every Presbyter should do it, would be committed to too many. *Both, indeed, are one and the same order.*" Similar confessions abound amid the works of the English divines of that age, which show how nearly they held our own views respecting the government of the church, and the equality of its ministers. "They maintain," says Prynne, "the doctrine of the parity of Bishops and Presbyters; declaim much against the pride, lordliness, ambition, domineering power, and other vices of prelates, and conclude that a bishopric is '*nomen operis, non honoris*—a name of *labour*, not of *honour;* a *work*, not a *dignity*.'" "Anselm, Archbishop of Canterbury," continues the same writer, in his Enarration on Philippians i. 1, resolves thus: "It is, therefore, *manifest by apostolic institutions*, that all PRESBYTERS are BISHOPS, albeit now those greater ones have obtained the title. For a Bishop is called an overseer, and every Presbyter ought to attend to the care of the flock committed to him.'" Here was evidently the early form of the primitive English churches. Each church had its Bishop. Nor when prelacy at length was fully developed did it prevent the reception of Bishops, who had been set apart by the laying on of the hands of Presbyters. The early Christians of Britain, while giving to the ministry a full estimate of its importance, regarded evidently the Episcopacy and the Presbytery of the early ages as essentially the same.

The early form of Christianity in Ireland was clearly Presbyterian; their Bishops, or Pastors, were chosen and supported by the people, and the historians of those primitive ages tell us that "*their churches were modelled, like all other apostolical churches, after the Jewish synagogue.*" The history of the introduction of the gospel into Ireland has become mingled with a thousand fabulous legends of St. Patrick, which are easily detected as the base impostures of a designing priesthood. Nor could they be received by any mind that had not already been brought into a blind and servile adherence to every dogma and tradition of men. But amidst this mass of superstition and folly there is a history which distinctly reveals the wonder of God's providence, and the power of his grace.

Near the city of Glasgow, in Scotland, at the close of the fourth century, Succathers, or Succat, afterwards called Patricius, and now St. Patrick, was educated by a pious mother in the knowledge of the truth. It is related that he was stolen by a pirate and carried to Ireland. There, in the fields, where he was set to tend swine, he recalled the lessons of heavenly wisdom he learned from his pious parents, and was converted to God.

"In that strange land," said he, "the Lord

opened my unbelieving eyes, and though late, I was converted with my whole heart to the Lord my God. The love of God increased more and more in me, with love and faith. The Spirit urged me to such a degree, that I poured forth as many as a hundred prayers in one day." Thus the truth began in his heart to work out what priestly power could never do. Afterwards, when restored to his country, he felt an irresistible desire to preach the gospel in Ireland. Returning thither, he carried with him the simple truths of God's word. He knew nothing of Romish traditions and priestly anointing. The Spirit had set him apart to the work.

Passing over those portions of Ireland, which were yet unblessed with the gospel, he established, it is stated, three hundred and sixty-five churches, ordaining the *same number of Bishops*, and three thousand Presbyters, evidently allotting, as we do, a Bishop or Pastor to each church, with a bench of Elders to assist in the government of the house of God, while he acted the part of missionary, and of presiding Presbyter. Protestantism and not Popery, Presbytery and not Prelacy, were plainly the form of early Christianity in Ireland.

Both in England and Ireland Popery was introduced, only after a long and bitter contest, in which every aggression it made was boldly and nobly disputed, until, true to its character, it wore out the saints of the Most High, and planted its blood-stained banner where first the standard of a pure and primitive Christianity had been the rallying point of the people of God.

The primitive church of Scotland was beyond a question essentially Presbyterian. During the second and third centuries many pious and learned men sought in that country a refuge from the fierce persecutions which the Roman Emperors were then waging against the church. Thus did Christianity shed its light upon that people long before Rome attempted to spread Prelacy among them. It was here that Succat was nurtured, who carried the gospel to Ireland and here for ages was carried on a most severe contest for truth, against the errors and corruptions of the Romish church. Towards the middle of the fifth century, Calladius was sent from Rome to introduce the Episcopacy of Prelacy into Scotland. "Before him, says an ancient historian, " the Scots were nourished in the faith by *Presbyters and Monks, without Bishops.*"

In the sixth century we find connected with the history of Scotland the Culdees, who appear to have fled thither from persecution. Their chief seat was the island of Iona, where was a theological seminary or monastery, wholly different, however, from the Catholic institutions which bear the same name. It was founded by Columba, an Irish Abbot, who took with him twelve Presbyters, over whom he had no superiority, except being their permanent Moderator. When he died, they chose a successor from their number, who became the presiding Abbot, without any additional rite of consecration. Similar institutions were founded over parts of Scotland and Ireland, having twelve presbyter-Abbots, and one permanent Moderator. They sent their missionaries over Europe, who went in all the simplicity of the gospel, carrying its blessings with them. They opposed all the novelties of Popery, which Augustine was then introducing into England. Their creed was *evangelical*, and their government *Presbyterian*. Bede makes for them this curious apology: "Having none to bring to them the Synodal decrees, by reason of their being so far away from the rest of the world, they therefore practised only such works of piety and charity as they *could learn from the prophetical, evangelical, and apostolical writings.*"

"Iona," says D'Aubigné, "governed by a simple Elder, had become a missionary college. It has been sometimes called a monastery, but the dwelling of the grandson of Fergus (Columba), in nowise resembled the Popish convents. When its youthful inmates desired to spread the knowledge of Jesus Christ, they thought not of going elsewhere for Episcopal ordination. Kneeling in the chapel of Icolmkill, they were set apart by the laying on of the hands of the *Elders;* they were called *Bishops*, but remained obedient to the *Elder* or Presbyter of Iona. They even consecrated other Bishops; thus Finan laid hands upon Diuma, Bishop of Middlesex. The British Christians attached great importance to the ministry, but not to one form in preference to another Presbytery and Episcopacy were with them, as in the primitive church, almost identical. Somewhat later we find that neither the venerable Bede, nor Lanfranc, nor Anselm—the two last were Archbishops of Canterbury—made any objection to the ordination of British Bishops by plain Presbyters."

Until the year 1109 the Culdee Presbyters ordained those who were called Bishops in Scotland. But the Papal power was gradually reducing their number and influence, until it wholly ceased, and Iona fell into the hands of the Augustinian nuns. But though their name became extinct, their principles lived and revived among the followers of

Jerome, and Huss, and Wickliffe, who, in the early dawn of the Reformation, maintained the pure doctrine of the word of God, protested against the errors that had corrupted the church, and taught that the order and discipline of the apostolic church was such as is now held by the great body of Protestant Christianity.

The facts thus briefly presented will serve to answer a question which is often asked with a sneer by the supporters of the Papacy and Prelacy: "Where was your church before the Reformation?" Its principles are found in the Bible, and they entered into the simple and popular government of the synagogue, and were the early type of the Christian church. All its grand outlines appeared amid those communities which have most purely kept the faith once delivered to the saints. It was found in the valleys of Piedmont, when all the world had gone after the lying wonders of the Man of Sin. It was the form which the Christian church first assumed in England, and Ireland, and Scotland, ere Popery had claimed those gems of the sea as its own. It is no new creation of wild Reformers, but is built upon the eternal truths of the gospel, and on the foundation of the apostles and prophets, Jesus Christ being the chief corner-stone. It has shone in ages of darkness with undiminished light. It has lived amid opposition, and persecution, and death. And when the morning of the Reformation dawned, it took its side, with the hosts of God's elect, against error, and superstition, and sin.

CHAPTER VIII.

THE REFORMATION.

THE Papal church had at length reached the lowest depth of its corruption, and darkness covered the earth, except where, amid the valleys of Piedmont, the light shone undimmed by all the growing superstitions of the age. The great doctrine of the gospel, "*By grace ye are saved through faith,*" had been lost amid a round of rites, and heartless observances, and unmeaning ceremonies. The priests of a corrupt religion had succeeded in inducing men to come to *them,* and not to *Christ,* for salvation, introducing *works* and *rites,* and *saints* between the sinner and the Saviour. Then a change of dress, a renunciation of social pleasure, and bodily comforts, and necessary food, and the pain of self-inflicted tortures, were substituted for *repentance* toward God. Afterward, as the Pope needed money, he began to sell *indulgences* for sin, and then to receive money for the redemption of souls from *purgatory.* Thus the church became a place of barter, and was full of corruption. Gradually it had thrown upon the people a burden of superstition which they were unable to bear. The Bible was laid aside, and the voice of tradition, speaking through wicked priests, became the guide of men. The visible church was changed from the bride of Christ to the "mother of abominations." The palace of the Popes was the scene of riot and crime—a cage of unclean birds. The clergy were ignorant and wicked—the people oppressed and borne down by an insupportable burden of superstition. A long night of darkness and sin rested upon the earth Yet, even in the midnight of the Papal supremacy, there were precursors of a coming day. The truth had its witnesses, and Christ was trusted and humbly worshipped by many who had been taught of the Spirit to know him aright.

Here and there a Bible was found, and its words gave life to the soul that learned to love them. In 1170 Peter Waldo, of Lyons, attempted a reformation, by calling the minds of his followers to the Scriptures. In 1360 Wickliffe arose in England, and translated the New Testament into English. He opposed the supremacy of the Pope, maintained *the equality of Bishops and Presbyters*, and taught that all human traditions in the church were superfluous and sinful.

Soon after John Huss, and Jerome of Prague,

were burnt at the stake for maintaining similar doctrines, and attempting to restore the Catholic church to the simplicity and purity of the apostolic age. It was the preparatory era, and Providence was arranging the materials with which, in another century, to introduce the Reformation.

The invention of printing provided the means of multiplying copies of the Holy Scriptures, and scattering truth like the light of heaven. The world was now ripe for a change, and God had prepared the men who were to be his instruments in its accomplishment. In every nation where the light of the Gospel was to make its way through the darkness of Papal superstitions, the Spirit was bringing minds in contact with the Bible, and sanctifying them through the truth.

In the beginning of the sixteenth century, Martin Luther, while studying law in the University of Erfurth, found a copy of the Bible in its library. The entrance of that word to his mind changed all his purposes of life. He became a monk. In his convent he found a Latin copy of the Holy Scriptures. This precious volume again was the object of his prayerful and constant study. His soul now became imbued with the truth. The errors of the church appeared in awful contrast to the simplicity of the gospel. At length he saw that the whole Papal system was opposed to Christ. His mind cast off every fetter, and he boldly stood forth for the defence of the truth as it is in Jesus. Powerful and learned men were sent to convince him of error; but he met and defeated them with the word of God. The Pope denounced him in solemn decrees, and he publicly burned them. He was summoned before kings and magistrates, yet he fearlessly defended the doctrines of the cross. He translated the Scriptures into his own language. The press, the invention of the preceding century, multiplied copies, so that the people could possess them. Then the truth spread over Germany, and the power of the Pope waned. The day began to appear. Many noble minds rose in defence of the truth, and heartily supported Luther in his work of reform. The principles of the Reformation advanced with the progress of the Bible. The entrance of that word gave light. It released the world from the superstitions of ages. It broke off the fetters of error and ignorance. It led the soul away from priests, and prelates, and rites, and saints, to Christ as the only means of salvation. The doctrine that we are justified by faith, was the power of God unto salvation. As it rose, the power of the priest declined.

Thus the Reformation commenced; but much

yet was to be done. In the long night of Papal darkness all the great doctrines of the word of God had been corrupted. One was needed who should arrange the truths of Christianity in their proper order and harmony, and present the great features of the gospel in such system, as might unite in closer communion the people of God, and resist the tendencies to fanacticism and error, which were growing out of that mighty revolution. Such a man was prepared by divine Providence, of whom it was said by a celebrated writer, "that he was the most exalted character that hath appeared since the days of the apostles, and at the age of twenty-two he was the most learned man in all Europe."

The name of John Calvin occupies an important position amid the Reformers of the sixteenth century, and is intimately connected with the history of the Presbyterian church. He was born at Noyon, in France, in the year 1509. His father intending him for a priest in the Romish church, gave him a liberal education, and secured for him a benefice from the Bishop of Noyon, at the age of twelve years. A few years after, however, having preached several sermons to the people of his native city, where he had been appointed a charge, his plans were broken up, and he was sent by his father to study law in the University of Orleans. "At my first entrance on that study," says Calvin, "I was indeed too pertinaciously addicted to the superstitions of the Papacy, to be easily drawn out of such deep mire. At length, however, having experienced some taste of the pure doctrines, I was inflamed with such zeal to progress further, that although I did not reject my other studies, yet I pursued them only in a cold and indifferent manner." Here he began to search the Scriptures, and as the truth broke upon his mind, he gradually withdrew from the Romish church. His varied talents and acquirements made him to be much sought after, so that his room had more the appearance of a public school than a private study. At the age of twenty-two he went to Paris, where he became acquainted with several persons of distinction, who had imbibed the principles of the Reformation. Here he prepared and published his first work, a commentary on Seneca's epistle concerning Clemency. He now devoted himself wholly to the cause of the Reformation, and publicly renounced the errors of Rome. As the storm of persecution was now raging fiercely in France, he retired to Basle, in Switzerland, where he published his great compend of Theology, the "Institutes of the Christian

Religion." After a brief visit to Italy, he was providentially directed to Geneva, where he intended to lodge but a single night, on his way to Noyon. Here he was made known to Farel and Viret, under whose labours the work of reformation had already been commenced in that city. Farel urged him to remain and share their toils with them, and when he seemed to hesitate, thus addressed him, "I denounce unto you in the name of Almighty God, that if under the pretext of prosecuting your studies, you refuse to labour with us in this work of the Lord, the Lord will curse you, as seeking yourself rather than Christ." Calvin dared not resist this appeal, but gave himself up to the disposal of the Presbytery and the magistrates, by whom he was elected preacher, and also appointed professor of divinity. He entered promptly upon the work assigned him. He *found the religious system and government of the church already commenced upon the Presbyterian plan,* and heartily approved it; and only endeavoured to perfect and establish it, by adding the bench of ruling Elders, in imitation of the Waldenses, and as he declared, expressly warranted by Scripture.

He drew up a Confession of Faith, and a Catechism for the better instruction of a people but just turning from the errors of Popery. While engaged in his work as a pastor and teacher, he sought not only to reform the doctrines, but the morals of the Genevese, and to introduce a healthful discipline in the church. Here he met with many evidences of the hostility of unconverted men to any true reformation, and with his associates was, by means of an unhappy faction, banished from the city. When informed of the decree of banishment, he said, "Certainly, had I been in the service of men, this would have been a bad reward; but it is well that I have served Him who never fails to repay his servants whatever he has once promised." Leaving Geneva amidst the lamentations of his flock, he visited Basle and Strasburg, where he was appointed professor of divinity, and planted a French church upon the Presbyterian model. Soon after his departure from Geneva, attempts were artfully made to bring that city back to the Catholic faith; but Calvin, who was informed of all that passed there, effectually put the people upon their guard against the wiles of their Popish enemies. While he was zealously engaged in his duties at Strasburg, an urgent call was made upon him to return to Geneva, and resume his office as pastor and teacher. At first he utterly declined; but afterwards, yielding to a sense of duty, was welcomed back by the people and senate, with every token of gratitude and joy. Here he remained until his death, which occurred on the 27th of May, 1564, in the 55th year of his age, and the 29th of his ministry. (See Note D.)

During this period he was engaged in incessant labours, both in public and in private. "In every fortnight," says Beza, "he preached one whole week. On Thursdays he presided in the meetings of Presbytery; on Fridays he collated and expounded the Scriptures to what we term the congregation. He was engaged in illustrating many of the sacred books, by commentaries of very uncommon learning. On some occasions he was employed in answering the adversaries of religion, and at other times wrote to correspondents from every part of Europe, concerning subjects of great importance." He died in the midst of his usefulness and labours, sincerely lamented by all who knew him best, and in the full enjoyment of a blessed hope through Jesus Christ our Lord.

His appearance is described by Beza, his companion and biographer, as follows: "His stature was of the middle size, his complexion dark and pale, and his eyes, brilliant even till death, expressed the acuteness of his understanding. His dress, neither highly ornamented nor slovenly, was suited to his singular modesty. He lived nearly without sleep. His power of memory was almost incredible, so that he could immediately recognize, after the lapse of many years, any one whom he had ever seen. His judgment was so sound and exact on all subjects, that his decisions seemed almost oracular; nor do I remember an instance of an error being committed by those who followed his advice."

The learning and genius of Calvin, combined as they were with an ardent piety and a sound judgment, gave him a prominent place in the Reformation. Perhaps there was no one in all that great struggle with error, whose counsel was so frequently sought after, or so readily received. The great work which Providence accomplished through him, was to *arrange* and *illustrate the system of doctrines taught in the Scriptures*, which had become almost forgotten, in the long night of superstition and error from which the world had just awoke. He devoted most of his energies to this work. From the time his mind first drank in the pure truths of God's word, he spared no expense of effort, and patient industry, to the elucidation of the doctrines of the Scripture. His labours were incessant. After he became a pastor and teacher, he preached or lectured on theology *nearly every day in the year.* His works, if all published, would form seventy octavo volumes. And these were prepared in the midst of his daily lectures, his constant pastoral duties, his controversies with the enemies of the truth, his varied correspondence with all the Reformers, the increasing feebleness of a body sinking under the severe tax upon its powers, and repeated domestic afflictions, which, but for sustaining grace, would have crushed him to the earth.

The system of doctrines which he taught in his works, and which are now styled Calvinism, is only a formal *arrangement* of the truths revealed in the holy Scriptures. Appearing, as they did, at a time when grievous errors and heresies were charged upon the Reformers by their enemies, his writings served to distinguish them from the fanatics who were then appearing, and to cement in a closer union the Christians of that age. In his theological opinions nearly all the Reformers agreed. For many years his "Institutes of the Christian Religion" were publicly studied, both at Cambridge and Oxford Universities, and when the Pope excommunicated the English church, one of his charges against the Queen was, *"that she received herself, and enjoined upon her subjects, the impious sacraments and institutes of John Calvin."*

The Protestant Archdeacon of Winchester, when brought before his Popish judges, in the time of the bloody Mary, said, "Which of you is able to answer Calvin's Institutions, who is minister at Geneva? *I allow the church of Geneva, and the doctrine of the same, for it is one, catholic and apostolic, and doth follow the doctrines which the apostles did preach, and the doctrine taught and preached in King Edward's day was also the same.* Many similar facts prove that the system taught by Calvin was received as truth by the Reformers of England, France, Germany, Switzerland, and the Netherlands.

They united in these doctrines, and contended for them. Wherever Popery was abandoned, there the truths which Paul and the apostles preached, which Augustine revived, which the Paulicians and the Waldenses believed, which Luther taught, and Calvin *only re-arranged*, were adopted as the great doctrines of the Reformation. And this was the work of this great man, to set forth in clear and distinct outline the instructions of God's word, and thus form a bond of union for the church of Christ. As to his connection with the Presbyterian policy, he only *perfected* what he already *found in existence.* When he came to Geneva, Farel and Viret had already been instrumental in establishing a Protestant church, and a Presbytery had been formed. *By that body Calvin was received as a minister, and appointed to the pastoral office.* He approved of all that had been done, and only perfected the work by appointing a body of ruling Elders, to assist in the government of the church. He showed the office to be in accordance with the teachings of Scripture and apostolic usage; and from this time the Presbyterian policy was, in more or less of its important features, adopted by all the branches of the church, except the English, which still clung to the institutions of prelacy.

The great work of the Reformation was now fully begun. The church had thrown off the burdens and deformities of the Man of Sin, and once more appeared in its original purity and simplicity. The restoration of the word of God to its proper place, *as the only rule of faith and practice*, opened the eyes of men to the errors which had crept in through the traditions of the fathers, and set them free from a long and oppressive servitude. The doctrines and principles of primitive Christianity were re-established. With wonderful rapidity they made their way over the nations of Europe. Wherever the light dawned, the influence of the Papal church waned. The power of God was revealed, owning his truth, and giving his word success. The crowning glory of the Reformation was the revival of the doctrines of the gospel, directing lost sinners to Christ as the only foundation, and calling them away from any dependence upon a round of heartless rites and unmeaning ceremonies. But with the restoration of the faith once delivered to the saints, there was also a return to the order and discipline of the primitive church. With very great unanimity the Reformers upon the continent advocated, and, as far as possible, introduced, the essential elements of Presbyterian government. The Lutheran churches, which were established under monarchical institutions, introduced an order of Presbyters, to whom were given prominent powers. But it was confessedly an act of simple *expediency*, and not because prelacy was regarded as sustained by Scripture authority. In a series of articles composed by Luther, as an abstract of the reformed faith, and signed by Melancthon and others, it was said: "It is clear, even from the confession of our adversaries, that this power (of dispensing the sacraments, discipline, &c.) is common to all that are set over the churches, whether they be called Pastors, Presbyters, or Bishops. Wherefore Jerome plainly affirms, that there is no difference between Bishop and Presbyter, but that every Pastor is a Bishop." The church of England was the only one that retained a form of government which denied the equality of the ministry, and required that prelatic order with which first began the corruptions of the Man of Sin. Its ministers were singularly passive during the early stages of the Reformation, and while Luther, Calvin, Knox, and others, who had once been priests of the Romish church, after their conversion took the lead in the struggle and directed the work, they allowed the monarchs and lords of the realm to fashion the English church so as best to support their own authority and supremacy.

Henry VIII., who at first opposed both Luther and Calvin, and received, therefore, the title of "Defender of the Faith," (though a monster of wickedness,) afterwards turned against the Pope because he would not sanction his divorce from his wife, and his marriage with another. When he had separated from allegiance to Rome, he assumed for himself and his successors the title of supreme head of the church of England. Thus clothed with spiritual as well as temporal power, he admitted reformation only to a limited extent. After the death of his son Edward, under whose brief reign the interests of true religion were greatly promoted, the "Bloody Mary" restored the Papist Bishops and Priests to power, and waged a cruel and merciless persecution against the supporters of the Protestant faith.

When Elizabeth came to the throne, the work of Reformation again advanced, and the truth gained rapid and glorious victories. Yet much of the pomp and show was retained, that entered so largely into the worship of the Catholic church. Nor was King James I., who followed her, disposed to aid the cause of true reform; and when urged by many of the ablest divines of his realm to permit the restoration of the doctrines, order and discipline of primitive Christianity, he gave, as his significant and memorable answer, "No Bishop, no King;" thus evincing his estimate of the harmony of prelatic and monarchical institutions, and paying a noble tribute to the tendency of Presbyterian principles towards a free government. Nor did facts fail to prove the correctness of his judgment. For when, after long and oppressive efforts to secure in the ministers of England a conformity to the rites and pomp of the established church, the Puritans became wholly separated therefrom, they formed a body, of whom Hume has said, "that the precious spark of liberty was kindled by them alone, and that to this sect the English owe the whole freedom of their Constitution."

It was doubtless owing to such circumstances as have been mentioned that the English church stood alone, among all the churches of the Reformation, in the support of prelacy. Yet while thus maintaining the order of the hierarchy, its ministers held for many years the most pleasant relations to the Reformers on the continent. The brightest ornaments of the church of England never dreamed of setting up their order and discipline as necessary to the existence of the church. They acknowledged the ministry of Geneva, and France, and Scotland, as may be abundantly proved. Archbishop Cranmer taught that in the beginning "*Bishops and Priests were but one office,*" and proposed courts like our Sessions and Synods. In the year 1582 the Archbishop of Canterbury gave license to John Morrison, who was *ordained by a Scotch Presbytery*, to preach in his province, ratifying that ordination, and pronouncing it laudable and proper. Many such facts show that while the early English Reformers retained Episcopacy, they cordially received and allowed the ministry made, as is ours, by "the laying on of hands of the Presbytery." The English Protestant church, therefore, stood alone in its adherence to the prelatical form of government, while the churches on the continent with great unanimity *affirmed*, and as far as possible *restored*, not only the doctrines, but the *order* of the apostolic age.

CHAPTER IX.

TESTIMONY—FROM SCRIPTURE—THE APOSTOLIC FATHERS—THE ENGLISH REFORMERS.

BEFORE passing to notice the history of the Reformed churches, which restored the features of the apostolic order and discipline, let us group together the various classes of testimony which prove that order and discipline to have been Presbyterial.

The first and most important witness, without which all other is of no value, is that of the holy Scriptures. Here is found the religion of Protestants. If our doctrines be not contained *there*, the whole testimony of tradition, the whole voice of the church, and the entire assent of the fathers to our claims, would give us no proper foundation on which to build.

The office of the ministry was established by Christ himself. The commission runs as follows:

"And Jesus came and spake unto them, saying, All power is given unto me in heaven and in earth.

"Go ye, therefore, and teach all nations, baptizing them in the name of the Father, and of the Son, and of the Holy Ghost;

"Teaching them to observe all things whatsoever I have commanded you: and, lo, I am with you always, even unto the end of the world. Amen." Matt. xxviii. 18—20.

In these words the apostles evidently were sent forth as *ministers*, whose chief duty was to preach the word and dispense the ordinances of religion. No especial power is delegated to them over any who may be associated with them in the work. No other order of ministers is mentioned. They had a special work as witnesses of Christ's resurrection, which ceased with them. But as ministers they claimed only to be simply Presbyters.

As we pass through the history of the church, as given in the Acts of the Apostles, we meet with two words, in constant use, as designating the same person—Bishop and Presbyter. The one referring to a duty, the other to an office or dignity. Thus in Acts xx. 17, 28, we read: "And from Miletus he sent to Ephesus, and called the Elders (Presbyters) of the church." After a long and faithful admonition he adds: "Take heed unto yourselves, and to all the flock over which the Holy Ghost hath made you overseers, (Greek,

Bishops,) to feed the church of God, which he hath purchased with his blood " The obvious testimony of this passage is, that Presbyters and Bishops were terms applied to the same rank or office.

In Titus i. 5—9 we read:

" For this cause left I thee in Crete, that thou shouldest set in order things that are wanting, and ordain Elders in every city, as I had appointed thee:

" If any be blameless, the husband of one wife, having faithful children, not accused of riot, or unruly.

" For a Bishop must be blameless, as the steward of God; not self-willed, not soon angry, not given to wine, no striker, not given to filthy lucre;

" But a lover of hospitality, a lover of good men, sober, just, holy, temperate;

" Holding fast the faithful word as he hath been taught, that he may be able by sound doctrine both to exhort and to convince the gainsayers."

In this passage are many important facts disclosed.

1st. It teaches us that a Bishop and Presbyter are one, else there is no force in the argument of the 7th verse, as showing the necessity of ordaining as Elders those who are described in the 6th.

9

2d. We see that there were several Bishops in a single city, and not one prelate claiming authority over his brethren. And

3d. We learn that the duty of a Bishop was simply that of any minister—to *teach* in the church (v. 9). Nor did the apostles claim any higher office than this, for in 1 Peter v. 1—2 the apostle writes: "The Elders which are among you I exhort, who *also am an Elder*, and a witness of the sufferings of Christ, and also a partaker of the glory that shall be revealed"—"Feed the flock of God, which is among you, taking the oversight (Greek, exercising the Bishopric) not by constraint, but willingly; not for filthy lucre, but of a ready mind." How plainly does this exhortation of the apostle teach the truth, that in the primitive church Elders and Bishops were one!

So, also, the apostle John claims for himself only the title of Elder. How strange is it that we no where meet with one declaration which asserts, what those who pretend to be their successors claim for them, that they held an office distinct from, and higher than that of the Presbyter. So strong is the testimony here, that Dr. Whitby confesses that both the Greek and Latin fathers do, with one consent, declare that Bishops were called

Presbyters, and Presbyters Bishops, in apostolic times, the names being then common. Notes on Philip. i. 1. And this is the only fair construction that can be put upon the terms as used in the Scriptures.

The testimony of the Bible is *evidently in favour of the parity of the ministry*, as now taught in the standards of the Presbyterian church, and wholly adverse to all prelatical claims as based upon the instruction of Holy Writ. It is equally evident that there was a plurality of Elders in every church. Thus in Acts xiv. 23: "And when they had ordained them Elders in every church, and had prayed with fasting, they commended them to the Lord, on whom they believed." Acts xx. 17, "And from Miletus he sent to Ephesus, and called for the Elders of the church." James v. 14, "Is any sick among you? let him call for the Elders of the church." Titus i. 5, "For this cause left I thee in Crete, that thou shouldest set in order the things that are wanting, and ordain Elders *in every city*." What does this and other similar testimony teach, but that then as now, *more than one Presbyter had rule in each church*. And this is confirmed by the known fact that the synagogue, after which the Christian church was modelled, was thus governed by a bench of Elders.

But were all the Presbyters of each church of the same class, or was there a distinction between teaching and ruling Elders? In Romans xii. 5–8 we read, among those who have received different gifts in the church are those who teach and those who rule.

"So we, being many, are one body in Christ, and every one members one of another.

"Having then gifts differing according to the grace that is given to us, whether prophecy, let us prophesy according to the proportion of faith;

"Or ministry, let us wait on our ministering; or he that teacheth, on teaching;

"Or he that exhorteth, on exhortation; he that giveth, let him do it with simplicity; he that ruleth, with diligence; he that showeth mercy, with cheerfulness."

In 1 Cor. xii. 28, we read, "And God hath set some in the church; first, apostles; secondarily, prophets; thirdly, teachers; after that miracles; then gifts of healings, helps, governments, diversities of tongues." Here we find among the officers of the church, "helps and governments," mentioned in distinction from the church, in which they are set.

In 1 Timothy v. 17, it is written; "Let the Elders that rule well be counted worthy of double honour, especially they who labour in word and doctrine." It is difficult to conceive how one can avoid the conclusion, that this text clearly divides Elders into two classes, ruling and teaching, especially when we remember that this answers to the government of the synagogue which the Christian church resembled.

The office of Deacon formed no part of the ministry, as is evident from the account of its institution, as given in Acts vi. 1—6.

"And in those days, when the number of the disciples was multiplied, there arose a murmuring of the Grecians against the Hebrews, because their widows were neglected in the daily ministration.

"Then the twelve called the multitude of the disciples *unto them,* and said, It is not reason that we should leave the word of God, and serve tables.

"Wherefore, brethren, look ye out among you seven men of honest report, full of the Holy Ghost and wisdom, whom we may appoint over this business.

"But we will give ourselves continually to prayer, and to the ministry of the word.

"And the saying pleased the whole multitude; and they chose Stephen, a man full of faith and of the Holy Ghost, and Philip, and Prochorus, and Nicanor, and Timon, and Parmenas, and Nicolas a proselyte of Antioch,

"Whom they set before the apostles: and when they had prayed, they laid *their* hands on them."

The *union* of separate churches under one body exercising oversight upon them, is taught in Acts xv. 1—4, 22—29, where an important question was decided authoritatively, by an ecclesiastical council, or Synod of Ministers and Elders, the representatives of the church.

The *ordination* of church officers is also represented to be the act of two or more pastors or ministers. Thus in Acts xiii. 1—3, we read the record of the ordination of Barnabas and Saul as follows:

"Now there were in the church that was at Antioch certain prophets and teachers; as Barnabas, and Simeon that was called Niger, and Lucius of Cyrene, and Manaen, which had been brought up with Herod the tetrarch, and Saul.

"As they ministered to the Lord, and fasted, the Holy Ghost said, Separate me Barnabas and Saul for the work whereunto I have called them.

"And when they had fasted and prayed, and laid their hands on them, they sent them away."

These two went forth together, establishing churches and ordaining Elders therein. So was

Timothy ordained by the "laying on of the hands of the Presbytery," and not by a single prelate. To the power then conferred by the united act of a council of Elders, was added the endowment of supernatural gifts (not belonging to the *office*, but essential to the early ministers of the gospel) by the laying on of the hands of the apostles. 2 Tim. i. 6. The "gift" here alluded to was evidently the power of working miracles. Or if it be regarded as referring to the ordination of the youthful Timothy, it but brings forth as a matter of history, the fact that Paul was a member and Moderator of the Presbytery by whom the solemn act was performed. Here then do we find the Scriptural warrant for Presbyterial order and discipline in the church.

How that order became early perverted and changed we have already seen. Yet, even amid those who in succeeding ages effected, or assented to those changes, we meet with witnesses who confirm the opinions which we form from the simple record of the Scriptures.

THE TESTIMONY OF THE FATHERS, though much resorted to, is of infinitely less moment than that of the Bible. They were but fallible men, and among them were found many fearful evidences that though living near the apostolic age, much of the apostolic spirit had died out from the church. Nor would it be any overwhelming argument against the truth of the doctrines maintained by the Presbyterian church, if not one witness among the Fathers could be found to sustain the record of the word of God. Here we rest with safety our claims to be a part of the universal church, and to possess all the prominent features of the apostolic model. Yet, even the Fathers, and especially they who lived nearest the apostles, testify to what we hold to be truth. Clemens Romanus, who lived toward the close of the first century, uses the terms Bishop and Presbyter interchangeably, evidently applying them to one and the same office. Thus he says, "For it would be no small sin in us should we cast off those from their episcopate (or bishopric) who holily and without blame fulfil the duties of it. Blessed are those Presbyters who having finished their course before these times, have obtained a perfect and fruitful dissolution. For they have no fear lest any should turn them out of the place, which is now appointed for them." Again, he rebukes in the church of Corinth rebellion against its Presbyters. Hermas speaks of the "Elders who preside over the church," and evidently regards "Bishops" and "Elders" as titles for the same office.

Polycarp, in his epistles to the Philippians, describes the duties of Presbyters and Deacons, alluding evidently to the same officers, whom Paul in his epistle to the same church addresses as Bishops. And he invests the Presbyters with all the authority that belongs to Bishops.

Ignatius, in his letter to the church of Magnesia, says, "Seeing then I have been judged worthy to see you by Damas, your most excellent Bishop, and by your worthy Presbyters, Bassus and Apollonius, and by my fellow servant Sotio, the Deacon, I determined to write unto you. I exhort you that ye study to do all things in divine concord; your Bishop presiding in the place of God; your Presbyters in the place of the Council of the apostles, and your Deacons, most dear to me, being entrusted with the ministry of Jesus Christ. But be ye united to your Bishop and those who preside over you." Many similar passages abound in the writings of this Father, which prove simply, that each church had its Bishop or teaching Elder, with a Council of Presbyters, and a Deacon to minister to the saints. The three classes of officers mentioned, belonged to each particular congregation. And moreover, the *Presbyters* are mentioned as the *successors of the apostles*.

Papias, who lived early in the second century, speaks of the apostles simply as Presbyters.

Irenæus gives most decided testimony in favour of Presbyterial order and discipline. He declares the "apostolical tradition to be preserved *through the Presbyters;*" and again speaks of the same tradition coming through the succession of Bishops, thus representing the apostolical succession, the Episcopal and the Presbyterian, *to be one and the same.*

Polycarp, Bishop of Smyrna, and a disciple of John, says, "Obey those Presbyters in the church, who have the succession, as we have shown, from the apostles, who with the succession of the Episcopate received the gift of truth, according to the good pleasure of the Father." Thus do these Fathers use the words Bishop and Presbyter as evidently applying to the same persons, and being identical. Nor do we meet with any evidence that any officer had authority over a collection of churches, as Pastor, all owing allegiance to him. The Bishops or Presbyters bore rule only over individual congregations.

When a change had taken place, as we have already seen, through the ambition of the ministry, we still meet with testimony which abundantly confirms the view we have taken of the apostolic order.

Thus, Ambrose, who lived in the fourth century,

writes as follows: "The apostle's writings do not in all things agree with the present constitution of the church, because they were written under the first rise of the church, for he calls Timothy, who was created a Presbyter by him, a Bishop, for *so at first the Presbyters were called.*"

Jerome declares, "Among the ancients, Presbyters and Bishops were the same."

Augustine writes: "The office of Bishop is above the office of priest, *not by authority of scripture*, but after the names of honour, which the custom of the church hath now obtained."

Chrysostom testifies as follows: "Having spoken of Bishops, and described them, Paul passes on to Deacons. But why is this? Because between Bishop and Presbyter there is not much difference; for these, also, in like manner, have committed to them both the *instruction and government of the church*, and what things he said for *Bishops, he intended also for Presbyters;* for they have gained the ascendency only in respect to ordination; and of this they seem *to have defrauded the Presbyters.*"

This passage is a fitting conclusion to the testimony of the Christian Fathers. It abundantly teaches, what we affirm, that in the apostolic age Bishops and Presbyters were identical.

The *testimony of the Reformers* may be appropriately introduced in this connection. What was the opinion of the Waldenses and the continental Reformers has already been apparent, and it were needless to reproduce their arguments in support of Presbyterial order. Let us glance briefly, therefore, at the sentiments often and plainly expressed by the prominent divines of the early English church, as forming a part of that testimony here grouped together.

Hooper, in a letter dated Feb. 1550, informs Bullinger, "that the Archbishop of Canterbury, the Bishops of Rochester, Ely, St. David, Lincoln and Bath, were sincerely bent on advancing the purity of doctrine, agreeing *in all things with the Helvetic churches.*"

Parkhurst, Bishop of Norwich, exclaims: "O, would to God, would to God, once, at last, all the English people would, in good earnest, propound to themselves to follow the church of Zurich, as the most absolute pattern."

Cranmer affirms, as his opinion, that "the Bishops and Priests were at one time, and were no two things, but *both one office* in the beginning of Christ's religion." He also proposed to erect courts, similar to the Kirk Sessions and Synods of Scotland.

Latimer and Hooper maintained the "identity

of Bishops and Presbyters by divine institution." Bishop Jewel assented to the same opinion, and expressed the hope that the "Bishops would become labourers, pastors and watchmen."

Dr. Willet, a divine of the church of England during the reign of Elizabeth, presents the following concessions: "That, therefore, which the apostles were especially appointed unto, is the thing wherein the apostles were properly succeeded; but that was the preaching of the gospel; as St. Paul saith, he was sent to preach, not to baptize. The *promise of succession we see is in the preaching of the word*, which appertaineth as well to other pastors and ministers as to Bishops."

Again he says: "Seeing, in the apostles' time, Episcopus and Presbyter, a Bishop and Priest, were neither in name or office distinguished, it followeth, then, that the apostles assigned no succession while they lived, neither appointed their successors; or that indifferently all faithful pastors and preachers of the apostolic faith are the apostles' successors." This concession of a distinguished Episcopal divine affirms fully the doctrine of our own church respecting apostolic succession.

Bishop Bilson delivers it as his opinion, that the "church was at first governed by a common council of Presbyters; that, therefore, Bishops must understand that they are greater than Presbyters rather by custom than the Lord's appointment; and that Bishops came in after the apostles' times."

Dr. Holland declares: "To affirm that there is such a difference and superiority, (between Bishops and Presbyters,) by divine right, is most false, contrary to Scripture, to the fathers, and to the doctrine of the church of England; yea, to the very schoolmen themselves."

Bishop Morton, in an address to Papists, tells them "that the power of order and jurisdiction, which they ascribe to Bishops, doth, by divine right, belong to all other Presbyters; and that to ordain is their ancient right."

Bishop Hall acknowledged the Presbyterian church of Holland to be a true church of Christ, accepted a seat in one of its most important Synods, and unequivocally acknowledged "that there was no difference, in any essential point, between the church of England and her sister Reformed churches." The only difference between us consists in our mode of constituting the external ministry; and even with respect to this point we are of one mind, because we all profess to believe that it was not an essential of the church, (though, in the opinion of many, it is a matter of importance to her well-being,) and we all retain a respectful and friendly opinion of each other, not seeing any reason why so small a disagreement should produce any alienation of affection among us."

A similar concession was made by Bishop Davenant, who also urged a fraternal union among all the Reformed churches, "declaring that they did not differ from the church of England in any fundamental article of Christian faith."

Archbishop Usher proposed a plan for the "reduction of the Episcopacy into the form of Synodical government, received in the ancient church." The essential principle of that plan is that Bishop and Presbyter were originally the same order; and that in the primitive church, *the Bishop was only a standing President or Moderator among his fellow Presbyters.*

Being asked by Charles I. "whether he found in antiquity that Presbyters alone ordained any," he answered, "Yes, and that he could show his majesty more, even when *Presbyters alone successively ordained Bishops,* and brought as an instance of this the Presbyters of Alexandria choosing and making their own Bishops, from the days of Mark till Heraclas and Dionysius."

Such are a few only of the witnesses of the

Reformation, as found in the church of England who testify to the Scriptural warrant of Presbyterial order, and who recognized those churches who returned to that order as a component part of the visible kingdom of Christ. How strangely such evidence from such men contrasts with the proud, uncharitable, and unchristian assumptions of many of their successors, who claim for themselves exclusively the title of *the church*, and to deliver all but themselves to the "uncovenanted mercies of God."

Here we may rest our evidence, praying that there may be again awakened that precious spirit of the Reformers, which shall recognize as Christians and members of the church, all who bear the image of Christ, and who hold the form of "doctrine once delivered to the saints."

CHAPTER X.

THE WALDENSIAN CHURCH.

THOSE ancient witnesses for the truth, that had for ages borne a noble testimony for the gospel, amid the valleys of Piedmont, deserve the first place in the history of Protestant Christianity. Though they have no claim to the distinctive title of a Reformed church, since they never became corrupted with the errors of Rome; yet they gave early evidence of their cordial attachment to the truths which were revived under the teachings of Luther and Calvin, and their co-labourers.

On hearing of the progress of the truth in Germany, two pastors, named George Morel and Pierre Masson, were deputed by the Vaudois churches, to visit the Reformers and confer with them on the great questions which were then agitating the Christian world. On learning what were the errors which the Reformers opposed, and the doctrines which they now received as truth, they assured them of their cordial agreement with them.

"We are,' said they, in an address to Œcolampadius, "the teachers of a certain unworthy and poor people. Yet in all things we agree with you; and from the very times of the apostles, our sentiments respecting this faith have been the same as your own." Thus cordially did this ancient church (never reformed, because never needing reformation,) give its fellowship to those churches which were shaking off their deformities and corruptions, and returning to the doctrines and order of the apostles, from which it had never swerved It forms, therefore, an important link in the history of the Presbyterian church, with whose principles it fully agrees.

Its early history, previous to the Reformation, has already been noticed. The persecutions which entered so largely into the experience of that people, were the results of the bitter and deadly hostility to the truth, ever manifested by the Papal church.

Cruel and bloody inquisitors, and equally rapacious and wicked princes, acting under the orders of the Pope, visited the Waldenses in their mountain homes, subjected them to ceaseless annoyances, destroyed their villages, expelled them from their valleys, closed upon them the doors of their dungeons, and lighted the fires of the stake, where many bore their dying testimony for Christ and his cause.

The historians of these events give accounts of thirty-two persecutions and invasions from their enemies, during which scenes of cruelty and bloodshed were enacted, the recital of which fills the mind with horror.

The following passages, from the Commission of Pope Innocent VIII. to the Archbishop of Cremona, show the fiendish spirit of him who professed to be the visible head of the church. "We have heard, not without much displeasure, that certain sons of iniquity, inhabitants of the province of Evreux, followers of the abominable and pernicious sect of malignant men, called the poor men of Lyons, or the Waldenses, who have long ago endeavoured, in Piedmont, and other neighboring parts, by the instigation of him who is the sower of evil works, to ensnare the sheep belonging to God—are damnably risen up under a feigned pretence of holiness, and do greatly err from the truth. We, therefore, having determined to use all our endeavours to root up and extirpate such a detestable sect, and the aforesaid execrable errors, and that the hearts of believers may not be damnably perverted from the Catholic church, have thought good to constitute you the nuncio commissioner of us, to the end you should induce the followers of the most wicked sect of the Waldenses, to abjure their errors. And that you may do this so much the more easily, you may admonish and require most urgently all Archbishops and Bishops seated in the duchy, whom the Most High hath called to share with us in our care, and command that they do assist you in the orders, and together with you proceed to the execution thereof against the forenamed Waldenses, and all other heretics whatsoever, *to rise up in arms against them*—and to tread them under *foot as venomous adders*, and bestowing all your care upon so holy and necessary an extermination of the same heretics." Acting under such direction, and armed with all the terrors of the Inquisition, and a brutal soldiery, the servants of the Romish hierarchy entered the peaceful home of the primitive church, and commenced a war of extermination against it.

Often were they bravely met amid the wild defiles of those mountains, and compelled to retreat before the stones and arrows which poured like hail upon them from the rocks which overhung their path. At one time an army of eighteen thousand were thus driven back. The scene of many of these fearful and wild contests is still visited annually by the youth of the Vaudois College, who there recall the history of their fathers, and in a few simple services keep alive the principles for which they contended and died, and render their thanks to Him who watched over them amid all their trials, and preserved them from utter destruction.

This defile is called the Barricade, and seems to have been thrown up by the hand of God as a refuge for his people, when called to stand against the fierce assaults of an enraged and brutal soldiery. In the year 1686 the Waldenses were expelled from their valleys, in the execution of a decree designed for their final extirpation. Out of fourteen thousand who were imprisoned, eleven thousand had already perished by cold, hunger, disease, and inhuman treatment. The remnant were compelled, in the beginning of an Alpine winter, to leave their homes and cross the mountains, exiles from all the scenes of their former joys and sorrows. In the course of their journey many perished from cold and exhaustion. Having halted over night at the foot of Mount Cenis, they pointed out to the Popish officer, who commanded them, a terrible storm, which had already commenced among the hills, and asked that they might remain under shelter until its fury was spent. But he refused their entreaties, and led them on through a tempest, in which the falling snow beat against them like pounded ice. Many of the exiles, already emaciated in body, and without sufficient clothing to protect them, sunk under the terrors of that memorable day. Mothers clasped their babes to their breasts, and found relief from their sorrows in death. One by one the feeble dropt off, unperceived by their companions, until eighty-six had perished in that fatal ascent. After incredible hardships, that band of exiles reached the Protestant cantons of Switzerland. Here they were received with a generous sympathy and with a warm welcome. But as the whole band at length came together, and inquiries were made from those who arrived first, of those who came last, the scene was such as to melt the bystanders to tears.

> "For all had lost some loved and loving one;
> Some fond and faithful heart—some friendly hand—
> That now lay bleaching on the Alpine snow."

The storm that had so long been gathering, had now spent its fury. The Papal church had manifested its bitter and unrelenting hostility to the people of God, and had become drunk with the blood of the saints. Every valley and hill had a voice and a story of outrage, wrong, and violence; and for three years the exiled Vaudois wandered amid the Protestant cantons of Switzerland. But, though receiving from that people unceasing tokens of kindness and sympathy, they could not forget their ancient homes. Like the Jews, by the rivers of Babylon, they wept when they remembered Zion, and her ruins were still precious in their eyes. They thought of those hills, where their fathers worshipped, hallowed by a thousand sacred memories of their mountain homes, now filled with their deadly enemies, and of their simple sanctuaries, now polluted by the mummeries of the Man of Sin.

At length they determined to regain their native valleys. Placing themselves under the care of M. Arnaud, who was both their pastor and commander-in-chief, a small, but determined, band of eight hundred men, with indefatigable perseverance, made their way through every obstacle, and manfully met every enemy, until they once more stood amid the scenes of their earliest and dearest recollections.

On the 16th of August, 1689, they set out upon their march, after having first commended themselves to God in solemn and united prayer. On the eighth day of their journey, they met and obtained a signal victory over an army of twenty-five hundred men, who had been stationed in one of the valleys to oppose their progress. On the 28th of August, they first regained possession of one of their churches, the old temple of Guigon. During the period of their expulsion it had been converted into a Catholic chapel, and was filled with crosses, the images of saints, statues of the Virgin, and like symbols of the Romish faith. Having removed these objects, that formed a part of the idolatrous worship of their enemies, they engaged in a solemn act of thanksgiving to God for his great mercies. The service was commenced by singing the seventy-fourth Psalm. After which, M. Arnaud, their pastor and leader, mounted a bench in the doorway, so that all might hear, and expounded the 129th Psalm. Both of these selections of Scripture will be seen, by referring to them, to have been singularly appropriate to their circumstances. Three years before, M. Leidet, the pastor of this church, had been detected in the act of private prayer, under a solitary rock. For this he had been dragged to a prison, and thence to a scaffold. His last words were: "Into thy hands, O God, I commit my spirit." Even the monks, who persecuted him, confessed that he died like a saint. The church, where he had preached Christ, was the first to be regained by the "eight hundred," on their "glorious return." A long series of dangers, and toils, and conflicts followed this signal victory ere that brave and devoted band once more repossessed their ancient valleys, and worshipped God as their fathers had done.

In the valley of St. Martin rises a monument of those struggles, ever memorable in the history of the Waldenses.

The hamlet which stands just upon the border of the wild mountain torrent that falls into the Germanesca, is Balsille, and high above it tower those stupendous and precipitous rocks that enter so largely into the scenery of the Waldensian country. The Rock of Balsille is a high conical hill, consisting of several terraces, with almost precipitous sides, from which a few straggling pine trees are growing. The approach to this natural fortress is through a wild Alpine gorge, in some points affording sufficient width only for a narrow pathway. Emerging from this pass the traveller comes to the hamlet of Macel, beyond which lies the village and rock of Ballsille. Here it was that Henri Arnaud and three hundred and sixty-seven exiles entrenched themselves against twenty-two thousand French and Piedmontese troops, and successfully resisted their assaults, driving them down the rocks with a frightful slaughter. During the winter of 1689–90 they dwelt among these wild fastnesses of the mountain, sleeping upon straw and leaves in the excavations which they had made in the rock, and living chiefly on roasted chestnuts, parched grains of wheat, and such other articles of nourishment as they could procure during the rigors of an Alpine winter. The history of the world presents few, if any, examples of greater courage and fortitude than were found among this brave and devoted band. It is worthy of especial notice, also, that Divine Providence had wonderfully prepared for their sustentation, by covering the wheat with snow when just ready to be harvested, thus preserving the grain in this unusual store-house, to be gathered by the exiles as they needed it for food.

On the 15th of May they retreated from their winter quarters, by sliding down a frightful ravine, leaving the French nothing but their vacant huts, while they passed on to a new position, and at length obtained full possession of their ancient homes.

Gradually the Vaudois families returned from their exile; the old churches were re-organized; the fields were again cultivated, and the hills and valleys were vocal with the praises of the Lord. Cruel edicts were once more enacted against them by Popish princes, who still bitterly hated them. But the providence of God watched over them, and preserved them from extinction. The English government became interested in their behalf, and often interposed for their aid. Queen Mary II., hearing of the destitution of their pastors, set apart twelve pensions for their support, and the various Protestant States of Europe gave many tokens of their sympathy. Thus they continue until the present day, hated by the Pope and Priests of the Catholic church, (ever true to its character in wearing out the saints of the Most High,) yet preserved by his power, who "causeth the wrath of man to praise him, and who restrains the remainder thereof."

The home of this people is wholly within the Alps. Five beautiful valleys, sheltered by these stupendous mountains, and extending in length twenty-two miles, and in breadth fifteen, form the country of the Waldenses. Their population is about 22,000. Their form of church government is Presbyterian. In each congregation is a Pastor, (formerly called a Barbe,) who is the Bishop of his flock; connected with him are a certain number of Elders, who assist him in the government and discipline of the people. The number of churches now existing is sixteen, of which fifteen are in the valleys, and one in the city of Turin.

These Pastors, together with the professors of the college at La Tour, and an Elder from each church, constitute a Synod, which meets once every three years.

A Moderator is chosen from the Pastors, who, with four other officers of the Synod, constitute a Table, (corresponding to our Boards,) by whom the business of the church is transacted during the intervals of the meetings of Synod. The government of the Waldensian churches is, therefore, strictly Presbyterial, and was so ages before the dawn of the Reformation.

Their public worship is conducted as follows. At the commencement of the service, after a brief invocation, the ten commandments are read, then a prayer, called *the confession*, is recited from their simple liturgy; after which a hymn is sung, then follows an extemporaneous prayer. After this the regent (a kind of village schoolmaster) reads the Scriptures, with comments. Then a sermon is preached, usually from memory, with extempore additions; then a prayer from the liturgy follows, and a hymn is sung, and the *creed* repeated by the minister alone. After the benediction, the congregation is dismissed with the request that in passing out they would remember to contribute at the door for the benefit of the poor.

As many of the people come from a considerable distance, the afternoon service follows the morning, with only a short interval.

Although the Waldenses are generally poor, they are liberal in their collections to aid in the spread of the gospel. And now, after ages of trial and persecution, they are called, in the providence of God, to a work for which they are peculiarly fitted, the spread of a pure Christianity among the people of Italy.

No other church could do for that country what they can. They appear before its inhabitants, not as a reformed, but as a primitive and apostolic church, whose history has been connected for centuries with that of Christianity in Italy. Hence, they who are convinced of the errors of the Papacy, look to them for the supply of the means of grace. Already, in Turin, beyond the valleys of Piedmont, a Vaudois church has been established, and Providence is evidently opening a large field of usefulness to that people, and calling them to enter and labour therein. Their Pastors are evangelical in their sentiments, and pure and blameless in their lives.

Their Confession of Faith accords with that of the Reformed churches of Switzerland, Holland, and Scotland. Of late years there has been a great increase of vital piety among the people. The labours of Felix Neff, about twenty-five years ago, were made, under God, the beginning of a good work, which has ever since been steadily advancing among them, and which has evidently fitted them for the solemn and momentous work to which they are now loudly called by Providence, the spread of the gospel throughout Italy. (See Note E.)

CHAPTER XI.

THE PROTESTANT CHURCH OF FRANCE.

EARLY in the history of the Reformation, the truths of the gospel began to awaken the people of France from the slumber of spiritual death. Towards the close of the fifteenth century, ere Luther had yet become disentangled from the maze of Popery, the light had dawned upon the minds of Le Fevre and William Farel. James Le Fevre was a learned doctor and professor of theology in the University of Paris. He had wearied of the study of relics, and the legions of saints, and had become disgusted with the corruptions of the Papal priesthood. He turned to the epistles of Paul, and there light broke in upon his heart. He had learned that we are justified by faith and not by works. Farel was his pupil. He, too, found the Bible, and "the entrance of that word gave light." Thus, even before the time that Luther began to shake the church by the preaching of the gospel, was the truth making its way for the Reformation in France, and the providence of God was aiding the work. In the court of Francis I. was found his sister, Margaret of Valois, afterwards Queen of Navarre, who had learned the truths of the gospel from Lefevre, Farel, and especially the pious Bishop of Meaux, who secretly favoured the Reformation. She gave her influence, and, as far as possible, her protection and assistance to the Protestant cause.

The jealousy of the Papacy was at length aroused, and persecution commenced. Farel found his way to Switzerland, where he spent the rest of his life, and, in conection with Viret, laboured in the work of reformation, in which Calvin afterwards joined him.

Here, with other friends of evangelical religion, he still sought the conversion of France. A printing press was established at Basle, from which Bibles and tracts were sent forth, through the generous aid of some rich merchants of Lyons. One of the first publications was Luther's exposition of the Lord's prayer.

On the 12th of October, 1524, an edition of the Bible was issued, and then the people had in their own language the precious word of God, with all its strong contrasts to the traditions of the Fathers. By means of poor but pious men, acting as *colporteurs,* these precious volumes were sold, from house to house, through many districts of France. The doctrines of the cross now made rapid progress. When once the people began to taste the waters of life, fresh from the fountain, they turned with loathing from the streams that came through the corrupted channels of human tradition and priestly superstition. And then the power of the Papacy waned, and persecution was used to force men back to the creed of the Fathers. Now the influence of Calvin was felt, whose writings were already convincing men everywhere of the truth. Thousands in France became converts to the reformed religion, and as churches were organized, they assumed the model already established at Geneva. Various names were given them by their Popish enemies, but that by which they are best known in history is Huguenot, the origin of which is uncertain, though it serves to distinguish a people whose name shall be held in everlasting remembrance.

The Reformation in France, which thus commenced under the simple influences of the gospel, was not forced upon the people by their rulers, but was the genuine result of the truth making its way to the hearts of men. When, therefore, a Protestant church was organized, it was formed upon the plan adopted by the continental Reformers, as resembling most nearly the apostolical model, and contained all the essential elements of Presbyterian order and discipline. Especial effort was made to secure, on the part of pastors, a faithful attention to the spiritual welfare of their people, and to disconnect them from all secular pursuits.

The first General Assembly was held in Paris, in the year 1559, one year before a similar body first met in Scotland. At this meeting, a Confession of Faith was drawn up, which resembles faithfully that of our own church, and embodies a distinct outline of the cardinal truths of the gospel, and presents a clear view of the order of the Presbyterian church.

Although persecution had already commenced, the cause of the Reformation made rapid progress. In the course of twelve years, 2150 churches had been established throughout France, some of which enrolled as many as 7000 members, among whom were found the noblest names of that age.

The growing strength of the Protestant cause at length awakened the bitter jealousy of the Catholic church, and drew from its leaders and priests their old arguments, the prison, the stake, and the sword.

Many had already borne witness with their blood to their love for the truths of the gospel. Scenes of bitter persecution had already tried the faith of the people of God, and served to illustrate their sincere attachment to the doctrines of his holy word. But now a new scene was to be introduced into the history of the Protestant church of France, written in blood, and memorable even amid the annals of violence and persecution.

During a long and severe struggle between the friends and the enemies of the Reformation, the Huguenots had obtained, at length, (as they supposed,) liberty of conscience and security from further wrong and outrage. Charles IX., King of France, in order to lull them into greater security, and thus prepare the way for the execution of his bloody purpose, declared that he was convinced of the impossibility of forcing men's consciences, and had determined to allow every one the free exercise of his religion. The Huguenot leaders were invited to Paris and loaded with favours. For two years this deception was practised, until all suspicion was allayed, and Paris was filled with thousands who had embraced the Protestant faith.

On the occasion of the marriage of Henry, the young King of Navarre, with Margaret, the sister of Charles IX., all the royal and noble persons who had professed the Reformed religion, were assembled at court to witness this pledge of mutual concession and reconciliation.

The whole plot was now ripe for execution, and sixty thousand armed men were collected in the city of Paris for its accomplishment.

St. Bartholomew's eve, August 24th, 1572, was set apart for the terrible scene which was henceforth to be memorable even among the dreadful acts of that apostate church, which is drunk with the blood of the saints.

The Admiral Coligny, the leader of the Huguenots, and the most pure of all their political men, had been previously wounded by a shot aimed at his heart by an assassin concealed in the house of a priest. But suspicion had been allayed by the promise of the king that the ruffian should be punished.

A little after midnight, on Sunday morning, at the command of the king and his queen mother, the deep vibrations of the cathedral bell awoke the city from its silence and repose, and gave the signal for the work of death.

The Duke of Guise, whose troops were already drawn up in the streets, led the way to the attack, while secret agents, who had been scattered throughout the city, awoke the Catholic population, to aid in the execution of their dreadful purposes.

The first victim of Papal hatred was the Admiral Coligny. The soldiers, entering his chamber, found him at prayer. The sight only inflamed their passion, and one of their number thrust his sword into his breast, while others, after mangling his body, threw it out of the window. The Duke of Guise, who was waiting to satisfy himself that the deed was done, wiped the blood from the face of the murdered Admiral of France, and having assured himself that it was he, gave a kick to the dead body, and exclaimed, "Lie there, venomous beast; thou shalt not spit thy poison any more."

Then turning to his soldiers, he bade them execute the work which had thus been commenced. At this same moment, the bell from the "Palace of Justice" sounded forth its summons, and with a shout of demoniacal triumph, the *massacre of St. Bartholomew* commenced.

At the appointed signal, every Catholic placed a light in his window, and a white cross upon his cap, and tied a white scarf upon his arm, as a means by which he might be distinguished from the "heretics."

Then the dwellings of Protestants were attacked; and by their infuriated murderers, they were dragged forth to death, amid the most appalling execrations, the groans of the dying, and the shrieks of men, women and children, who were seeking in vain for shelter or for mercy. The streets ran with blood, and were clogged with heaps of dead and mutilated bodies.

The Duke of Guise, the prominent actor in this horrid scene, ran about among the people, crying, "Blood-letting is good in August! Kill! kill! the king commands! For the king! O Huguenot!" The king himself beheld the awful spectacle from a window of the palace, and, with a frantic and fiendish joy, looked upon the piles of dead that were carried by to be thrown into the Seine, while the ladies of his court amused themselves with looking at the bodies of those slain in the palace, whom they had but lately met at the feast of the preceding day. Never before had such a scene been witnessed. Sixty thousand men in arms, were hunting down, like wild beasts, their own brethren, with whom they had but a few hours before been on terms of apparent intimacy and friend ship.

The work of death went on for seven days, during which time five hundred of the noble names of France, and ten thousand men of humble rank, perished, and were made the monuments of the bitter and undying hatred with which the Papal church regards the truth and its supporters

Nor was the massacre confined to Paris. Throughout France the same brutal scenes were enacted. And so well had the plot been laid that sixty thousand were numbered among the victims of that fatal day.

The news of these unparalleled atrocities was received at Rome with the liveliest demonstrations of joy.

The Cardinal of Lorraine rewarded the messenger who came with the tidings, by a gift of ten thousand crowns. At Lyons, the Pope's legate, who met the murderers fresh from the scene of butchery, absolved them from guilt by making over them the sign of the cross. At Rome, the Pope, with all his Cardinals and bishops, walked in a triumphal procession. Gregory XIII., so far from weeping over these dreadful scenes, congratulated the king on the accomplishment of an exploit "*so long meditated, and so happily execu'cd, for the good of religion.*" He ordered, also, triumphal medals to be struck, of which the engraving on page 136 is a copy:

On one side is a likeness of the Pope, with the inscription, "Gregorius XIII. Pont. Max. An. I.," and on the other is a destroying angel, with a cross in one hand and a sword in the other, executing the work of death upon the Protestants,

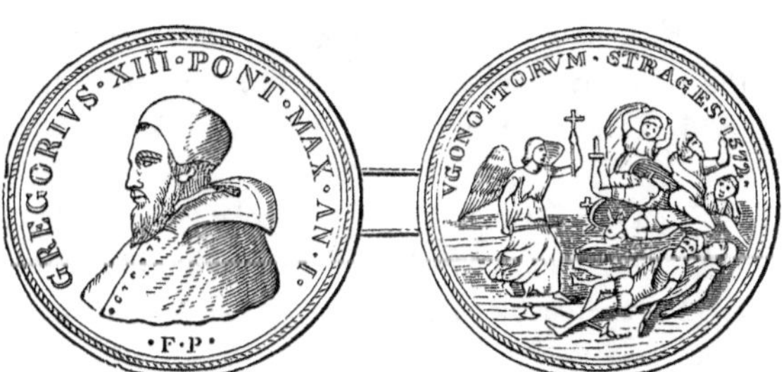

with the motto "Ugonottorum Strages, 1572," (the slaughter of the Huguenots). Thus has Rome perpetuated her shame, and given her full assent to the act by which thousands of innocent and blameless Christians were put to the sword.

The massacre of St. Bartholomew's inflicted a fearful blow upon the Protestant church of France, from which it never fully recovered. For six years the annual meeting of the General Assembly was discontinued. The leading friends of the Reformed religion were destroyed, the people were left exposed to the malice and violence of those who sought their extinction, and the number of churches was reduced to less than one thousand. At length, after a period of twenty-six years, Henry IV., a son of Marguerite, the Protestant Queen of Navarre, became king of France, and, though himself an apostate from the faith in which he was educated, he gave, under title of the Edict of Nantes, the first effectual protection to his Protestant subjects. This was in the year 1598.

From this time the Huguenots again rallied and strengthened, until, under the reign of Louis XIII., encroachments began to be made upon their privileges, and persecution to revive, followed at length by the Revocation of the Edict of Nantes in the year 1685. That act scattered the Protestant church of France, and sent forth thousands of her noblest sons to seek for that freedom of conscience in other lands, which they could never hope to enjoy under the dominion of the Papal church.

Many of them found refuge on the shores of the new world, and assisted in laying the foundations of the Presbyterian church of America.

From the time of this cruel act of revocation, until the time of Napoleon, the Protestant churches of France seemed to be almost extinct. Since then their cause has been reviving, so that now they are established upon the same general plan, with the churches of Scotland, Holland and America. They enjoy a measurable degree of toleration, though often made to feel that the Catholic priesthood still regard them with bitter hatred. Among their pastors are many sound and faithful ministers of the word, who are engaged in earnest and self-denying efforts to spread once more, throughout France, the blessed truths which can alone make that people happy and free.

CHAPTER XII.

THE REFORMED DUTCH CHURCH.

EARLY in the history of the great struggle between truth and papal error, the doctrines of the Gospel began to make their way amid the inhabitants of the Netherlands. While the old nobility and the prelates of the Catholic church adhered to the established religion, the principles of the Reformation made their way among the mass of the people and the inferior clergy, and though compelled to struggle against bitter persecution, obtained a final and glorious triumph. The Netherlands were an assemblage of separate States, under the dominion of Spain, whose monarch, at this period, was Philip II., an intolerant and bigoted subject of the Pope, who determined to extirpate the Reformed religion by the most violent methods.

The dark and bloody Inquisition was therefore established, and some of the noblest men of Holland became its victims; yet, amidst the fearful engines of papal cruelty, thus established, the truth rapidly made its way. A Confession of Faith, drawn up after the model of the French Calvinistic church, was adopted in the year 1561.

In the year 1566 the first public meeting was held, in an open field, by a converted monk, named Herman Stricker, under whose bold and powerful displays of truth an audience of seven thousand persons was assembled. His example was followed by others, throughout the province, until the doctrines of the Gospel were openly preached in the cathedrals, from which the Roman Catholics were expelled in the year 1573, at which time the Reformed religion was publicly established in Holland.

After the United Provinces had achieved their independence of Spain, (first declared in 1581, and attained after a long and desperate struggle,) they made rapid advances in commercial and political prosperity; while the Reformed Church of Holland assumed a distinguished position, for the devotedness and zeal of her pastors, and the eminence and learning of her theologians.

The form of government adopted was fully Presbyterian, and the articles of faith wholly agreed with those of Geneva and France. Yet, while this became the established religion of the new Republic, it was distinctly announced by the Prince of Orange, the Stadtholder, or President, "that he should not suffer any man to be called to account, molested, or injured for his faith and conscience." Thus early did the principles of Presbyterianism begin to work out political and religious liberty; and Holland deserves the honour of leading the way for the full and perfect development of the Protestant faith.

It was to be expected that when they renounced the despotic rule of Philip, they should also prohibit the public exercise of the spiritual despotism under which the nations of the earth had long suffered,—by whose mandates the choicest blood of Holland had been shed. Yet, while it was forbidden to make any public exhibition of Popish superstition, it was also declared that there was no intention "to impose any burden, or to make inquisition into any man's conscience," nor "to build up living temples to the Lord by force and by external arms," and "that no princes or magistrates *had authority over the consciences of their subjects in matters of religion.*"

Such were the noble sentiments sent forth under the influence of the Presbyterian church in Holland. While the people, and their ministers and rulers, loved the system of doctrine which had now become the established religion, they extended to others the same liberty of opinion which they had demanded of Philip, and in behalf of which they made a noble and successful effort. Thus Holland became the home of liberty, and the asylum for the oppressed. Occasionally religious differences assumed an asperity and warmth that formed an exception to this; yet no nation has more generally acted out this great principle of religious liberty. There the exiled Jew found a home; there the Puritans of England obtained "freedom to worship God," and found a place where they might rest, until ready to seek a home amid the wild forests of America. There bigotry and intolerance were rebuked, the world received a noble lesson in political and religious liberty, well worthy its imitation, and principles were established and acted out, which set forth the Reformed church of Holland as a pillar of the truth, and the noble and fast friend of that freedom which we most value, and which alone springs from the pure doctrines of the word of God.

The Reformed church of Holland has ever been the firm supporter of that system of doctrines which Calvin set forth in his works, as the sum of truth taught in the holy Scriptures. In the year 1562, Guido de Bres, a native of Belgium, who shortly afterwards suffered martyrdom, wrote a Confession of Faith, which he submitted to Calvin and others, and of which they approved. This series of articles, now called the Belgic Confession, was adopted by the early Synods of the church, as embodying their views of divine truth.

In the year 1563, Ursinus and Olivianus, by the order of a German Elector, prepared a Catechism, which was published simultaneously in the German, Dutch, and Latin languages. From the fact of its being framed at Heidelberg (in Germany) it is called the Heidelberg Catechism, and has been incorporated with the standards of the church of Holland, as presenting all the important points of Christian doctrine.

The canons of the Synod of Dort, also, are received as authority, and contain a distinct account of the leading principles of the Presbyterian faith. This Synod was the result of a long and painful controversy, which arose in Holland in consequence of the erroneous instructions of Arminius, a professor of theology in the University of Leyden.

Though entering upon his duties in that institution with the solemn promise to teach nothing but the "received doctrines of the church," (a pledge to which he for a while adhered,) he began privately to attack some important points of the established creed, and at length made an open and bold denial of those articles of faith which are specially connected with the sovereign purposes of God, in the work of salvation. In these rising difficulties the States at length interfered, requiring the courts of the church to report their proceedings to them, and to reverse a sentence of suspension, which had been pronounced upon several ministers, who withheld their assent from the articles of the received doctrine. Then the dispute became political, though the Synod of Holland disregarded the repeated commands of the State.

In the year 1609 Arminius died. But the unhappy contest was continued by his followers, who, from a formal remonstrance which they presented to the States of Holland, are called the "Remonstrants." To settle these disputes, the Synod of Dordrecht, or Dort, was assembled. The idea of such an assembly was suggested by James I. of England, in a friendly letter to the States General. Afterwards it met with favour by Maurice, the Prince of Orange, and head of the United Provinces. The Synod accordingly met at Dort, (a city of South Holland,) on November 16th. Delegates from all the provincial Synods were appointed in the proportion of four ministers to two ruling elders. Representatives were present from the churches of the Palatinate, Switzerland, Bremen, England, Scotland, &c. The Episcopal church of England was represented by the Bishop of Llandaff, the Dean of Worcester, and others, thus giving its sanction and the tokens of its fellowship to this important council of the Presbyterian church. The Synod continued through more than seven months. It was composed of eighty-six members, men of undoubted piety and learning, brought together to discuss and decide upon matters of the highest importance to the interests of the church. In the course of its deliberations, the Heidelberg Catechism and the Belgic Confession were ratified as part of the standards of the Reformed church, and the Remonstrants, or Arminians, declared to be heretical disturbers of the church and nation. There were acts connected with these decisions which at the present day appear in painful contrast to the general principles of liberty, so nobly maintained in Holland. Severe enactments were made, and intolerant proceedings were allowed, which that people could not be induced to repeat at this day. Yet, it must not be forgotten, that the Remonstrants were in error in continuing to claim the character and privilege of the members of the Reformed Dutch church, when they openly denied its doctrines. Had they honestly separated from a body whose tenets they could not receive, they would doubtless have been permitted to enjoy the same privileges which were accorded to other denominations.

Yet, even with the most impartial admissions of the harshness and severity of the decisions of the Synod of Dort, and of the measures which followed, we cannot but wonder how far in the advance of the age were the Presbyterians of Holland, in their ideas of religious toleration, and in the freedom which was enjoyed among them. Emerging as they were from the darkness and superstition which had rested upon them, under the dominion of the Romish faith, they threw off, by a noble effort, the chains of error, and guided by the truths of the gospel restored their church to the apostolic model, and gave to their nation the pure doctrines and the enlightened freedom of which the Bible is the only source.

The Reformed Dutch church whose history has been briefly described, forms an important branch of the Presbyterian family. Its officers are ministers, elders and deacons, and its judicatories or courts are the Consistory, (composed of the officers of a single church,) the Classis, (consisting of all the ministers and lay delegates of a certain district,) and the Particular and General Synod. These courts correspond to the Session, Presbytery, Synod, and General Assembly of the Presbyterian churches of Scotland and America. The elders and deacons are elected for a term of years, at the expiration of which they cease to act, unless re-elected. But they are never re-ordained, and are still regarded as church officers, forming what is called the Great Consistory, which is sometimes called together to decide on questions of vital importance to the interests of the congregation.

Early in the history of American colonization, the Dutch church was planted here, the simple model of a republican government, which more than a century after was almost exactly imitated in the formation of our own political institutions. Its founders were emigrants from Holland, where they had been trained under Christian influences, and taught to value the Holy Scriptures and the ordinances of the sanctuary. There they had learned the great lesson of religious toleration in an age of bigotry and persecution. It was in Holland that the Puritans, driven from their own land by the intolerance of an established Prelacy, had received from a government under Presbyterian influences, shelter and sympathy. There they had seen in the state, the first practical workings of a system which embodied the grand outlines of Presbyterianism, confederation and representation, and which was thus essentially republican and self-governing. The colonists, who came from thence, brought with them the church of their fathers.

As early as 1626, a place of worship was erected near the first fort built in New York. Here they met at first, and heard the Scriptures and the Creed read upon the Sabbath, by two church officers called 'Krank-bezoekers,' or 'visitors of the sick.' In 1633, a clergyman was sent out from the Classis of Amsterdam, by which body the Dutch church was supplied with ministers until the year 1757, when independent judicatories were established. It is worthy of notice that the earliest recorded efforts to teach the Indians the religion of Jesus, were made by the Pastor of the church at Fort Orange, (now called Albany.) In the year 1643, several years before the labours of Eliot in behalf of the Indians began, Dominie Megapolensis had interested himself in their behalf, and often had them among his hearers when preaching the gospel, and had frequent opportunities of explaining to them the nature and elements of the Christian religion.

For more than a century the Dutch churches of America received their pastors from Holland, and were subject to the jurisdiction of the Classis of Amsterdam. The necessity of a separate organization at length became apparent, and after a long discussion, independent church judicatories were established, in consequence of which an unhappy division took place, which lasted for many years, and seriously threatened the existence of the church. Under the influence of Dr. Livingston, who returned from Holland, where he had been to prosecute his theological studies, in the year 1770, the separate parties were united, and the church has since moved on harmoniously. Until the year 1764 divine service was performed entirely in the Dutch language. After this the English was introduced, and is now universally used.

The church has besides its various boards of missions, &c., a College and a Theological Seminary. The attention of its people was early awakened to the importance of establishing means for the proper education of young men for the ministry. In 1770 Queen's College, afterwards called Rutgers, was founded at New Brunswick; in 1784 a Theological Professor was chosen, and in 1810 the first Theological Seminary in the United States was established near the college, under the patronage, and by the efforts of the Reformed Dutch church.

Thus did the Presbyterianism of Holland early extend itself in this country, identifying itself with its interests, and seeking to promote them by establishing the means of religious instruction, and general education. She brought with her the same toleration in matters of faith she had left at home. One of the noblest testimonies borne to the liberal and Christian principles of the early Dutch settlers of this country, was by a Jesuit Father, who had been won by their kindness to speak well even of those whom he regarded as heretics. While the Dutch church was for years the established religion of New York, those who were persecuted and driven out from other colonies, found here a shelter under its influence. It has thus ever set a noble example of Christian liberality, while at the same time it has firmly maintained the truth, and resisted to its utmost the encroachments of error. It has cordially united with other evangelical churches in all their great enterprises, which have been established for extending the knowledge of the truth, while also ardently loving that form of doctrine, and order of the church, which, in all its essential features, was first delivered to the followers of Christ.

CHAPTER XIII.

THE CHURCH OF SCOTLAND, FROM THE REFORMATION TO THE FIRST GENERAL ASSEMBLY.

HAVING traced thus far the progress of the Reformation, in restoring to the church its primitive order and beauty, we are brought to notice the history of that work in Scotland. The early form of Christianity in that country, as has already been stated, was Presbyterian. The Culdees, of whom mention has been made, after a long struggle against the encroachments of the Catholic heresy, were finally suppressed, at the close of the thirteenth century. Their last public documents bear the date of 1297. But it cannot be supposed that their principles were lost. In the succeeding century mention is made of those whom the Pope denounced as heretics, and who, it is believed, still kept alive the faith that an apostate church desired to crush.

The doctrines of Wickliffe found a reception among those who still honoured secretly the faith of the Culdees. In 1407, John Resby was burned for maintaining tha: "the Pope was not a Vicar of Christ, and that no man of a wicked life should be acknowledged Pope." In 1432, Paul Craw, a Bohemian, a follower of John Huss, was burned for denying the doctrines of transubstantiation, auricular confession, and praying to saints.

Meanwhile the Popish priesthood were seeking to strengthen their power and influence, unaware for a time that the spirit of religious inquiry had not been suppressed by the murder of those who openly maintained the truth. At length, awaking to the fact that many minds were shaking off the shackles of error, especially in the west of Scotland, they summoned about thirty persons before a council, on the charge of heresy, in denying the arrogant claims of the priesthood, and the worship of saints and images. By the interposition of James IV. they were dismissed without any punishment.

Early in the 16th century the writings of the continental Reformers began to be read, and prepared the way for the wondrous work which developed throughout that kingdom the Presbyterian church of Scotland. One of the first to feel the power of those truths that were shaking the world was Patrick Hamilton, a youth of royal extraction, and of noble intellectual and moral endowments. Having been designed for the church, he made such progress in his studies as to excite the jealousy of the ambitious but ignorant priesthood, and partly to avoid them, yet more to study the doctrines of the Reformed faith, he visited the continent, and sought and enjoyed the friendship of Luther and Melancthon. Here his mind became fully open to the truth, and the chains of Papal error were for ever broken. On his return to Scotland he publicly preached the doctrines of the gospel.

Multitudes followed him to listen to his instructions. His learning, his eloquence, his youthful appearance, and his deep and earnest love of the truth, gave him at once a commanding influence, which soon called for the usual Papal arguments, the faggot and the stake. But his growing popularity made it necessary to act with caution. Accordingly he was first decoyed to St. Andrews, on the pretence of having a free conference with the Catholic clergy on the doctrines of the church. After obtaining a full avowal of his belief, he was apprehended at night, and committed to the castle. The next day he was brought before his Popish judges and condemned. In front of the college of St. Salvador the pile was erected, on which he was to give his final testimony to the truths of the gospel Here, after having been scorched by an explosion of powder, he continued to pour out his heart in prayer. A priest who stood near him exhorted him to call upon the Virgin Mary; but was answered by a solemn rebuke, and a warning to remember the judgment. The flames now kindled upon him, yet, amid that awful scene, his voice was heard distinct and calm, "How long, O Lord, shall darkness cover the realm? How long wilt thou suffer this tyranny of man? Lord Jesus, receive my spirit." Thus died this youthful martyr, at the age of 24, Feb. 28, 1528. From that hour the truth spread with wonderful rapidity. The means used to suppress it were most successful in extending it. Some of the friars began to preach doctrines which the worldly and wicked priesthood could not receive.

Threats of further burnings were made, to which it was replied, that if the Archbishop burned any more he had better do it in cellars, "for the smoke of Mr. Patrick Hamilton hath infected as many as it blew upon." Such was the dawn of the Reformation in Scotland. The day was now rapidly approaching, and was soon to arise in a brightness which no human power could dim. God was bringing to pass his glorious purposes, and none could stay his hand, or say, What doest thou?

The death of Patrick Hamilton was the beginning of a long and bitter persecution of the friends of the Reformation. The principles for which he perished were daily gaining ground. Alexander Seaton, the king's chaplain, plainly taught that we are justified by faith only, and that remission of sin lies not in the power of man, but is to be obtained by sincere repentance, and a cordial reception of Christ as our Saviour. Many of the clergy cast away their idle legends, and preached the "truth as it is in Jesus." Learned men felt the influence of the gospel, and yielded their hearts to its control. In February, 1538, five men were condemned and burned in one pile at Edinburgh. Of this number four were ministers, one of whom (Dean Thomas) had been called before his Bishop for preaching from the Epistles and Gosples, and desired to forbear. It was added, however, that if "he found a *good gospel* or *good epistle* that made for the liberty of the 'holy church,' the Bishop willed him to preach that, and let the rest be." The Dean replied, "that he had read both the New Testament and the Old, and that he had never found an *ill epistle* or an *ill gospel* in any of them." "I thank God," answered the Bishop, "I have lived well these many years, and never knew either the Old or the New. I content myself with my portuise and pontifical; and if you, Dean Thomas, leave not these fantasies, you will repent when you cannot mend it."

But the threats and persecutions of the hierarchy could not prevent the progress of the Reformed doctrines. Truth was everywhere making its way into the minds and hearts of men. The Bible, already translated into the language of the people, was imported by merchants from England, and circulated, by proper and prudent agents, with untiring industry. Several families would possess a copy in common, and meet at night to read and talk over its sacred revelations. Its entrance gave light, even before the voice of the living ministry had been heard proclaiming and enforcing its precepts.

In the great change that was taking place many of the Scottish nobles were included, and boldly enrolled their names among the earliest friends of the Reformation. Thus did He, who has the hearts of all men in his hands, prepare the way for that successful struggle which was soon to take place, in which even the political power of the Papacy should be destroyed.

The bloody spirit of the Papal priesthood was also fast alienating the minds of the people from a religion which sought to sustain its influence by the death of those who loved the truth, and whose pure lives displayed its power. Thus were events ripening for an open rupture between Scotland and Popery. In the year 1546, a tragedy was enacted which seemed to awaken to a new life the cause of the Reformation. Two years before, George Wishart returned to his native land, after a few years' exile, for having taught the Greek language at Montrose. Immediately he began preaching the Reformed doctrines. His high attainments as a scholar, his earnest devotion to the truth, his fervent piety, his modesty and meekness, combined with most commanding powers of eloquence, drew after him crowds both of the nobility and of the common people. His preaching was attended with wonderful success. When shut out from the churches by the orders of the Bishops, he preached in market places, or upon the hill side, yet followed by the same throng, who trembled as he reasoned with them of righteousness and judgment, and who wept at his tender displays of the love of God in Christ. But he, too, was destined to add a new name to the victims of Papal persecution. At the instigation of Cardinal Beaton, he was arrested and condemned to be burnt. The sentence was executed in presence of the Cardinal, who looked upon the scene from one of the windows

14

of the castle of St. Andrews. When led to the stake, Wishart kneeled down and prayed: "O, thou Saviour of the world, have mercy on me! Father of heaven, I commend my spirit into thy hands." Then rising, he addressed the people, exhorting them to believe and obey the word of God. The executioner, who begged forgiveness for the deed he was to do, he kissed upon his cheek, saying, "Lo, here is a token that I forgive thee; my heart, do thine office." At the sound of a trumpet the fire was kindled, and his sufferings commenced. To one who drew near to cheer him, he said, "This fire torments my body, but no way abates my spirit." Then, looking towards the Cardinal, he uttered the prophetic words, "He who, in such state from that high place, feedeth his eyes with my torments, within a few days shall be hanged out at the same window, to be seen with as much ignominy as he now leaneth there in pride." Thus died this noble witness for the truth. Within three months his death was fearfully avenged upon the author of it, who, in his own castle, fell under the hands of conspirators, without one word of penitence, finishing up a life of ambition, licentiousness and cruelty, crying, "I am a priest, I am a priest! fie, fie, all is gone!"

The death of Wishart was followed by the introduction of one to the work of the Reformation, whose name "will be had in everlasting remembrance." This was John Knox, the great Scottish Reformer.

The history of John Knox holds a prominent place among the records of the Reformation in Scotland. He was born in the year 1505, and at the age of sixteen entered the University of Glasgow, where he enjoyed the instructions of John Major, a man whose opinions on civil and ecclesiastical government were singularly in advance of the age in which he lived, while at the same time he defended many of the grossest follies of the Papal system. After having received the degree of Master of Arts, Knox taught Philosophy for a while with great success, and was then advanced to priest's orders, even before arriving at the canonical age for entering the ministry. The Reformed doctrines had been preached with considerable success before the mind of Knox embraced them. But it was impossible that in the general agitation of opinion then going on he could remain long unaffected. Under the preaching of George Wishart his mind was especially aroused, and became fully possessed of the truth. The change in his sentiments was soon apparent, and awakened the jealousy of the

Catholic priesthood. In the year 1547 he entered the castle of St. Andrews, then in the hands of the friends of the Reformation, when he was publicly called to preach the gospel. Though, for his new views of truth, he had been deposed by the Papal hierarchy, he regarded this as a proper call to exercise the functions of the ministry. John Annan was, at that time, chaplain to the castle, and it was through him Knox was thus introduced to the great work which lay before him. When he was thoroughly convinced that Providence had set him forward for the defence of the truth, he at once boldly proclaimed the church of Rome to be Antichrist. From that time there was no possibility of a compromise between the friends and the enemies of the Reformation. The work was of necessity thorough. It shook off not merely the outward trappings, but the whole system of Popery, and retraced all the steps by which it had departed from the simplicity and purity of the Primitive church. It retained neither its *doctrines* nor its *government*. It brought the church of Scotland to the simple platform of the synagogue, with its Bishops, Elders, and Deacons for every assembly. But this great change was not accomplished without a long and severe struggle with the Man of Sin. Unable to effect their purposes without foreign aid, the Scottish prelates procured the assistance of France, ever ready to lend her armies for the support of Papal authority.

Under their assaults, the defenders of the castle of St. Andrews were obliged to capitulate, and were taken to France and confined to the galleys as slaves. Among them was John Knox. Frequent efforts were unsuccessfully made to convert the prisoners to the Catholic faith. It is related by the Reformer, that one day a fine painted image of the Virgin was brought into the galleys, and a Scotch prisoner was desired to give it the kiss of adoration. He refused, saying that "such idols were accursed, and he would not touch it." "But you shall," replied one of the officers roughly, at the same time forcing it towards his mouth. Upon this the prisoner seized the image, and throwing it into the river, said: "Let our Lady now save herself; she is light enough, let her learn to swim." The officers with difficulty saved the image from the waves, and the prisoners were relieved for the future from such troublesome importunities.

In the month of Feburary, 1549, after an imprisonment of eighteen months, Knox was released, and permitted to return home. He immediately repaired to England, where he soon began to preach the doctrines of the gospel with great success. In the year 1551 he was appointed one of the chaplains to King Edward VI. His influence was such that during the revisal of the Book of Common Prayer he was consulted, and obtained an important alteration in the communion-service, completely excluding the notion of the bodily presence of Christ in that sacrament. He also assisted in the revisal of the Articles of Faith in the English church.

In the year 1553 Archbishop Cranmer, by the direction of the council, offered him the vacant living of All-Hallows, in the city of London. But he declined it, because of the present state of the English church, in which "there were many things that yet needed reformation." Afterwards the king, with the concurrence of his council, offered him a *bishopric*, which he also rejected, because "the Episcopal office was destitute of Divine authority in itself, and its exercise inconsistent with the ecclesiastical canons."

These facts, while they evince the noble adherence of the Reformer to what he believed to be truth, show the estimation in which he was held by the ministers of the English church in that age, and that they regarded him as a minister of Christ, truly and properly ordained to his office. This was the man whom Providence had introduced to the great work of the Reformation in Scotland.

The Protestant cause, which rapidly advanced during the brief reign of Edward VI., received a severe blow at his early death. Many of the English ministers would gladly have brought their church back to the apostolic model; and the king himself was evidently in favour of a more perfect reformation of the church than actually was accomplished. But the accession of Queen Mary restored the Papacy to power, and introduced a scene of persecution that has stamped her name with infamy. At first Knox was unwilling either to desist from preaching or to leave the kingdom; but at length was prevailed upon to retire before the storm, and not expose himself needlessly to the rage of his enemies. Accordingly, he visited Geneva, where he made the friendship of Calvin, and devoted himself to study. At length he returned to Scotland, in the year 1555, and recommenced his labours. Many of the nobility gathered around him, and threw the weight of their influence in favour of the cause of the Reformation. The queen regent sought, by every means, to retain the Catholic ascendency, but her efforts only increased the zeal of the Reformers. On the 3d of December, 1557, those of the nobility who were devoted to the interests of the Reformation subscribed a covenant, engaging to each other mutual support in the defence of the gospel. The chief subscribers to this article are called the *lords of the congregation*, from the repeated occurrence of the latter word in the document to which they affixed their names. Between them and the Papal authorities commenced a long and severe struggle, which was only terminated when the nation became wholly Protestant.

The queen regent, having openly manifested her determination to suppress, by any means, the Reformed doctrines, had brought to her aid the French troops; the Protestants sought, and at length obtained, aid from Elizabeth, then Queen of England. When it was seen by the French court that the English were determined to defend the cause of the Reformers, their armies were withdrawn on the 16th of July, 1560. On the 1st of August the Scottish Parliament assembled to deliberate upon the condition of the country. A petition was introduced, praying that the anti-Christian doctrine of the Papal church be discarded, and that the *order and discipline* of the *primitive church* be restored. In answer to the first part of the petition, several ministers, among whom was John Knox, were appointed to draw up a summary of Christian doctrine. The Confession of Faith was afterwards read and adopted, and on the 24th of August, 1560, the Parliament abolished the Papal jurisdiction, and rescinded all the laws which had been made in support of the Roman Catholic church.

Under these new arrangements, ministers were appointed to preach in the larger cities; and for the large country districts superintendents were provided, who were to supply the place, for the time, of a settled ministry. There was no difference in their ordination and that of the settled pastors; and to avoid a false conclusion from the appointment of such officers, when it was proposed to make the Bishop of Galloway superintendent over the district in which he had exercised his bishopric before it was abolished, he was rejected, "lest the appointment should give colour to the idea that the office was Prelacy under a different name." After the labours of the Parliament were ended, the Reformed ministers and leading Protestants met at Edinburgh on the 20th of December, 1560.

This was the First General Assembly of the church of Scotland. It consisted of forty members, six of whom only were ministers. Having already adopted a Confession of Faith, they applied themselves to the work of drawing up a book of discipline. In the plan they marked out they endeavoured to follow the plain lessons of Scripture.

The permanent officers of the church they arranged into four orders, viz: the minister or pastor, the doctor or teacher of theology, the ruling elder, and the deacon. To these they added, as temporary officers, because of the paucity of ministers, superintendents and exhorters. This latter class consisted of pious persons of ordinary education, who were appointed to read for their more ignorant neighbours who could not enjoy the instructions of the sanctuary. If they continued to improve in their ability to impart spiritual knowledge they were finally admitted to the ministry.

The government of the church was vested in the hands of the pastor and session. Presbyteries were also erected, which, with the Provincial Synods and a General Assembly, constituted the courts of the church. Such was the result of the Reformation in Scotland. Unlike that of England, it was thorough, shaking off not only the unscriptural doctrines, but the antichristian order of Popery. It restored the *bishop* to the position assigned to him by the Scripture, the care of a particular congregation. It re-established the simple faith and discipline of the apostolic church. It was commenced and carried forward by men and ministers converted by the truth from the errors of popery. The church was itself reformed. Its *foundation* and *identity* remained. It had only cast off its deformities, and once more appeared in its ancient simplicity and glory.

CHAPTER XIV.

THE CHURCH OF SCOTLAND—FROM THE FIRST GENERAL ASSEMBLY TO THE ADOPTION OF THE LEAGUE AND COVENANT

The history of the church of Scotland, after the meeting of the first General Assembly, presents for many years a series of fearful struggles with the Papal hierarchy. The princely revenues which had been attached to the office of bishop, were a golden prize which the crown and the nobility desired to retain, even at the expense of truth and the peace of the kingdom. Hence constant efforts were made to force upon the church an office which, with great unanimity, had been decided by the Reformers of Scotland and the continent to be wholly without a Scripture warrant. In this struggle John Knox bore a conspicuous part. Even before Queen Mary he boldly and firmly maintained what he believed to be truth, unmoved either by her threatenings or her persuasions.

In the year 1560, a dark cloud seemed to hang over the church. A league had been formed by Popish princes for the entire extermination of the Protestants in France and the Low Countries, and the complete destruction of the Reformed doctrines throughout Europe. In this detestable conspiracy, Mary, Queen of Scots, was ready to join. The Popish clergy were to be restored to all their former political power, and the altars of a corrupt faith to be again erected in the churches from which they had been banished. Everything seemed to favour the plan. Some of the leading Protestant lords were in exile, and the enemies of the truth were looking forward to an easy triumph. But the hand of Providence averted the blow that was about to fall on the church. Rizzio, the Italian favourite of the queen, and who was the secret manager of the dark intrigues of the Catholic princes, was assassinated at the instigation of the king, between whom and Mary a fatal alienation had taken place. This deed was followed by a series of unwise and criminal acts on the part of the unhappy queen, which resulted first in her confinement at Lochleven castle, and eventually in her melancholy death. The regency, during the youth of her son, James VI., was conferred on the earl of Murray, who threw his whole influence in favour of the Protestant cause, and in a noble and bright example of Christian statesmanship, earned for himself the title of the "Good Regent."

Under him the church of Scotland gained strength, and was legally recognized as the national church, not as receiving its existence and power from human authority, but from its divine Head; and only placed in a position of safety from its enemies by the act of government, which ratified and confirmed the work of the Reformers. The noble attitude assumed by the regent, drew upon him the malice of the Papal priesthood, and the hand of an assassin was employed to remove him out of the way. Hamilton, nephew of the Archbishop of St. Andrew's, was the instrument used to accomplish the act. Though by that very man his life had once been spared in battle, he coolly followed him from place to place, until a favourable opportunity occurred for the commission of the deed. He deliberately shot him from a window, as he was passing through a crowded street. It is worthy of record, that while the friends of the regent, around his dying bed, were lamenting that he had spared the life of his murderer, he replied that nothing "should ever make him regret having done a deed of mercy."

The death of Murray, which occurred in 1570, was followed by a renewal of efforts to restore the prelacy to power. It had been allowed the Popish prelates to retain two-thirds of the revenues attached to their benefices, during their lifetime, although they were no longer recognized as a part of the national church. As these benefices became vacant, the nobility desired to seize them for their own use, yet dared not, by such a glaring violation of law, add a new element of strife to the fearful struggle by which the country was already excited. The Earl of Morton first devised the scheme by which the difficulties might be obviated, which seemed to prevent the accomplishment of their selfish desires.

Upon the death of the Archbishop of St. Andrew's, he obtained permission to dispose of the Archbishopric and its revenues, and accordingly nominated one with whom he had made a previous arrangement, that he should enjoy the title and give to him the emoluments. This wicked transaction opened the way for great corruption, against which the church had to contend. The nobility, anxious to enrich themselves, desired to retain the hierarchy, giving to them certain superintending powers only, and making them subject to the authority of the General Assembly. During the discussions which followed this proposition, John Knox began to sink under his long and exhausting labours. In the month of September, 1572, the news of the massacre of St. Bartholomew reached Scotland. The Reformer was conveyed to the pulpit, where, in the presence of the French ambassador, he pronounced the vengeance of "heaven on that cruel murderer and false traitor, the king of France." On the 9th of November he preached at the installation of his successor, at Edinburgh, and having closed the services, walked down the street, "which was lined with his audience, who, as if anxious to take the last sight of their beloved pastor, followed him until he entered his house,* from

* The edifice stands at the head of "the Nether-bow," near the High Street, Edinburgh (old town). A considerable space stretches in front, where a large concourse might assemble, and from the upper window the Reformer was used to pour forth his eloquence without fear, favour, or affection. At the corner may be seen his bust, of rudest stone, in the most artless sculpture, and near it a triple inscription of the name of God, in Greek, Latin, and English. The several apartments have been rented to different tenants; but behind tnese is a redeeming trace, more sublime in its associations than the mark of the bloody hyssop on the lintel and doorposts of Israel; immediately over the door, in the strong and simple language of the time, is written:

"LUFE . GOD . ABOVE . ALL . AND . YOUR . NIEHBOUR . AS . YOURSELF."

which he never came out alive." His death was peaceful and holy. November 24, 1572, he sunk to his rest in a full and blessed hope in Christ. On the 26th, he was buried in the churchyard of St. Giles. His remains were followed to the grave by the regent Morton, by all the nobility of the city, and by a vast concourse of people.

As his body was laid in its last resting-place, the regent, as he looked thoughtfully and sadly into the sepulchre, pronounced his eulogy in the simple and truthful words, "Here lies he who never feared the face of man."

The death of John Knox was followed by a most desperate effort to force upon the church of Scotland that form of ecclesiastical government, which it had firmly resisted as wholly without a scriptural warrant. The regent Morton, a bold but unprincipled man, desirous to enrich and strengthen himself, secured the appointment of bishops, against which the Assembly firmly remonstrated. In this crisis appeared Andrew Melville, after an absence of ten years from his native land. He had spent much time in Geneva, with Calvin and Beza, and his influence was at once felt in the great contest which was now in progress. The Archbishopric of St. Andrew's was offered, as a bribe, to induce him to support the usurpations of the prelacy, but the base attempt proved ineffectual. Threats were tried, but equally in vain. "There will never be quietness," said the regent, "in this country, till half-a-dozen of you be hanged or banished." "Tush, sir," replied Melville, "threaten your courtiers after that manner. It is the same to me whether I rot in the air or in the ground. The earth is the Lord's. My country is wherever goodness is. I have lived out of your country two years as well as in it. Let God be glorified; it will not be in your power to hang or exile his truth."

It was thus that the church of Scotland withstood the efforts to destroy its power and purity. In 1578, the regent Morton resigned his office, and King James formally assumed the crown. The General Assembly now perfected its form of government, by adopting a new and carefully arranged book of discipline. It also ordained, that in future no new bishops should be made, and that the existing bishops should submit themselves forthwith to the General Assembly, under pain of excommunication. The bishop of Dunblane, who was present, immediately yielded assent to their commands. Two years after an act was passed, declaring the prelatic office wholly without scriptural authority, and requiring all who held it to lay it aside. So great was the power of the Assembly, that in the course of the year all but five of the "pretended bishops" relinquished their power, and submitted to the act which abolished Episcopacy throughout Scotland. In 1592 an act of Parliament was passed, which ratified the constitution of the church, and has ever since been regarded as its great charter, by which its sacred authority was legally recognized and confirmed But although King James had publicly professed his love for the church, and in a meeting of the Assembly had declared his determination to live and die in it, when, by the death of Queen Elizabeth, in 1603, he had become king of England and Ireland, he soon expressed his partiality for that form of ecclesiastical government which has ever proved more congenial to royalty, and better fitted to uphold its authority, than the republican simplicity and equality of the Presbyterian church. Then commenced another long and shameful effort to re-introduce prelacy into Scotland.

What else could be expected of a man who had seriously written a work to sustain, among other propositions, "that no man is more to be hated of a king than a proud Puritan; that Puritans have been a pest to the commonwealth and church of Scotland, have sought the introduction of *democracy* into the State, and quarrelled with the king because he was a king, and that parity in the church should be banished, Episcopacy set up, and all who preached against bishops rigorously punished." One of his first acts of aggression was to interfere with the General Assembly, seeking wholly to suppress its meetings. And when delegates from several Presbyteries came together, in accordance with the charter already granted, the king sent orders to proceed against them with the utmost rigour. Fourteen of the most eminent ministers were sent to prison, among whom was John Welch, the son-in-law of John Knox. Six of these were, after trial, convicted, and after suffering fourteen months' imprisonment, were banished to France. Such was the commencement of the royal attempt to force Episcopacy upon Scotland.

In the year 1618, a General Assembly was called at Perth, by the orders of the king, for the purpose of securing the triumph of his favourite measures. They met in the Little Kirk, in which was a long table in the centre, and benches on each side of it. At the head were his majesty's commissioners, and around the table the nobility and prelates, newly appointed by the king, while the ministers were left to stand behind them. Spotswood claimed the moderator's chair as bishop of that diocese, and then the Dean of Winchester was introduced, who read a letter from the king recommending the adoption of five articles, which introduced *kneeling at the communion—the observance of holidays—episcopal confirmation—private baptism—and the private administration of the Lord's Supper.*

When the haughty prelate, Spotswood, who had appointed himself moderator, called for the decision of the question, it was in the words: "Will you consent to these articles, or will you disobey the king?" And he declared that whoever voted against them should have his name transmitted to his majesty. But even then many remained firm to their principles; and forty-five ministers, with two other delegates, voted against the change. By a formidable and corrupt combination, these articles were adopted, and on the 4th of August, 1621, the Parliament summoned for the purpose ratified and confirmed them. At the very hour when the deed was being announced, a terrific storm burst over the city, as if to mark, with the frown of heaven, the act of treason against the King of kings. This day, known in the annals of Scotland as the "*black*

Saturday," was the beginning of a series of bitter trials to the church, which only ceased when that whole people, aroused to a noble and manly resistance, obtained, by a united effort, freedom to worship God.

King James I. of England had at length succeeded in the partial overthrow of Presbytery in Scotland, by means which must for ever stand as a dark blot upon his name, and which were alike dishonourable to the friends of prelacy. through whom he accomplished the act. Yet it will be noticed how the monarch and the prelates, by whom he sought to carry out his purposes, recognized the church of Scotland, with its *ministers and courts*, as a branch of the church of Christ, and acknowledged its right to make its own internal arrangements. The faithful ministers of the church struggled against the newly-risen power of the prelates, refusing them obedience, and resisting and denying their authority. When, however, the sanction of the Parliament had been given to the acts, which for a time defaced the external beauty and order of the church, the infatuated king and his imperious prelates determined to enforce submission, even by the most arbitrary and cruel measures. One of the first who was made to feel their oppressive power was John

Welch, who had been banished for fourteen years from Scotland for his manly resistance of kingly usurpation. His wife, the daughter of John Knox, obtained an interview with the king, and besought permission for her dying husband to return to his native air, as the only hope of restoring his failing health. His majesty, with coarse oaths, refused permission, except she would persuade him to submit to the bishops. "Please your majesty," replied the noble matron, at the same time holding up her apron, "I would rather receive his head there."

When the king heard that Welch was near to death, in cruel mockery he sent him permission to preach. The opportunity was unexpectedly embraced. The dying man went forth once more and proclaimed the gospel, and then returning to his chamber, in two hours after fell asleep, and passed away to his eternal rest. Robert Bruce, who also nobly resisted the change in the polity of the church, was first imprisoned, and on his release, confined to Inverness and its environs. But his punishment became a blessing to that people, among whom he faithfully declared the truth as it is in Jesus.

Similar measures were resorted to with all the prominent ministers of the Scottish church. Even the people did not escape. The change which had been temporarily effected met with little favour among them. And many disgraceful scenes occurred even at the communion-tables, from the attempts which were made to enforce a compliance with the article, which required them to kneel at the Lord's Supper.

The seminaries of learning were also attacked. Those who still adhered to the principles of the Presbyterian church were removed from office; and candidates for the ministry, who would not subscribe to the five articles of Perth, were rejected. But, during this period of darkness and distress to the church, the more pious and faithful ministers and their adherents quietly met together, and gave themselves to prayer. The light of the Reformation was not yet quenched. At Edinburgh there arose a strange controversy, which served to strengthen the popular feeling against the measures of the prelatic party. At one of their meetings between the kirk session and people, complaint was made that Mr. William Forbes, recently appointed pastor of one of the city churches, had taught that there might be easily effected a reconciliation between the church of Rome and the Protestant churches. The friends of Forbes and of the prelacy applied for an order to try those citizens who had expressed disapprobation of his doctrines. The order was given, and as the result of the trial, one of the magistrates of Edinburgh was deposed from office, and imprisoned until he should pay a ruinous fine; and five other citizens were either imprisoned or banished from the country. The death of King James, in the year 1625, put a period, for a time, to these despotic and disgraceful measures, and gave a momentary relief to those who had suffered thereby.

But the accession of Charles I. was soon followed by new attempts completely to destroy the Presbyterian church, and to establish prelacy upon its ruins. It was his wish to assimilate in all respects the churches of Scotland and England. Hence he attempted to introduce a liturgy, which had never been used regularly in the Scottish worship, and to abolish the control which had hitherto been exercised over ecclesiastical affairs by the lower courts of the church.

The efforts which were made to bring back the church of Scotland to the prelatic order and discipline, and to the ceremonies and forms of worship which the people regarded as only an imitation of the pomp and rites of the Papacy, soon awakened a spirit throughout the nation which no human power could resist. Petitions were drawn up and presented to the king, but no redress was given; and it soon became apparent that the most desperate measures would be resorted to, to force that system upon the nation which it had so unanimously and sternly resisted. Edinburgh, the early home of the Reformation in Scotland, was made a bishopric; and Mr. Wm. Forbes, already suspected of an undue leaning to Popery, was appointed the first prelate. He immediately ordered all the Presbyteries within his diocese to conform to this new measure. Some submitted, but others refused to comply, and boldly warned him of the sin of thus wantonly aggrieving the consciences of the people, by measures for which they could find no warrant in the word of God. But the earnest protest of the wisest and best men of the nation was of no avail in arresting the designs of the king, and his ambitious and tyrannical prelates. A liturgy was prepared and revised by Archbishop Laud, who made it as near as possible like the Popish mass-book. This was ordered to be used in the churches. A burst of popular indignation followed, which was felt throughout Scotland. The first experiment at enforcing this act was made in Edinburgh, when a riot, evidently the unpremeditated result of outraged feeling, followed. Everywhere there arose a stern determination to resist these attempts to introduce Papal and prelatic order and pomp, as undermining and destroying all their religious liberty. A despotic letter from the king, re-enforcing previous acts respecting the liturgy, only roused the people to a manly resistance. The whole kingdom was awakened from its lethargy.

It was now apparent that the king was determined to force upon them, at any hazard, the system which they believed to be both unscriptural, and subversive of all civil and religious liberty; and they determined never to bow their necks to a yoke which neither they nor their fathers could bear. They resolved, therefore, solemnly to renew the covenant into which the nation had once entered, "to put away all idolatry, superstition and immorality, and to worship God in simplicity and faithfulness, according to his word." Accordingly, a *covenant* was prepared, and on the 28th of February, 1638, was subscribed first at Edinburgh, and then throughout Scotland. The first public convention for this purpose was held in Grayfriars church. An immense crowd filled both the building and the churchyard. After prayer, the Earl of Loudon explained the object of the meeting, and exhorted the people to put their trust in the strength of God.

Mr. Johnston then unrolled the parchment, on which Scotland's new covenant with God was written, and read it in a firm and clear voice. An aged nobleman, the Earl of Sutherland, first affixed his name to that momentous document, after which it was signed by all within the church, and then carried into the churchyard, where it was spread out, and speedily filled with names. Thence it was sent over the city, and copies were circulated and signed throughout the kingdom.

In the month of November of the same year in which this covenant was framed, a General Assembly was held, by the permission of the king, who now saw the futility of any attempt to force prelacy upon the church of Scotland. After a noble and successful contest with the prelates, who were still unwilling to relinquish their power, acts were passed which annulled the Assemblies of previous years, which had changed the government and corrupted the worship of the church. The National Covenant was also approved, and the *Five articles of Perth* abjured. Thus did Scotland once more vindicate her rights, and acknowledge the sovereignty of Christ as alone the Head of his church.

The General Assembly, when it had closed its solemn and important deliberations, adjourned to meet the next year at Edinburgh. Its closing services were impressive. Addresses and admonitions were made by the elder and more venerable members of the body, after which prayer and praise were offered, and the apostolical benediction was pronounced, and the Assembly dissolved in these words—"*We have now cast down the walls of Jericho; let him that rebuildeth them beware of the curse of Hiel the Bethelite.*"

As might have been expected, the acts of the General Assembly awakened the deep displeasure of the king, who resolved to invade Scotland with an army, to enforce a conformity to his wishes, and to bring the church to submission. A system of defence was promptly commenced by the Covenanters; and when the army of Charles entered Scotland, it found itself opposed by a body of stern and determined men, willing to peril their lives in the defence of the truth. When the king perceived the strength and resolution of the Scottish army, he assented to a treaty, by which the struggle was for the time peacefully terminated, and permission given to hold a General Assembly, to which all ecclesiastical matters were to be referred for jurisdiction. This Assembly met, and again condemned those prelatic invasions which had disturbed the peace of the church, though it expressed the highest regard for the king. But the opposition manifested to his favourite form of church government was deemed an act of disloyalty to him, and again the note of preparation for war was heard, and the king determined to reduce the church to subjection by the force of arms. A severe struggle followed, which was attended by the most important results in both kingdoms. England, as well as Scotland, began now to see the necessity of uniting, for the preservation of civil and religious liberty. A treaty was formed between the English Parliament and the Scottish army, and a "Solemn League and Covenant" was signed, for the preservation of the Reformed religion of the church of Scotland, and for the reformation of religion in England and Ireland, according to the word of God. Connected with this act was the meeting of the "Westminster Assembly," in the year 1643, to whom the church is indebted for the admirable compend of religious truth, contained in the Confession of Faith, and the Larger and Shorter Catechisms.

The execution of Charles I., while it terminated a long series of oppressive acts against the civil and religious liberties of his people, opened a new scene in the history of the church of Scotland, which fully tested its faith and Christian principle, and love of the truth as once delivered to the saints.

CHAPTER XV.

THE CHURCH OF SCOTLAND—FROM THE DEATH OF CHARLES I. TO THE FORMATION OF THE FREE CHURCH.

On the death of Charles I. of England, Oliver Cromwell became Protector of the commonwealth, and conducted the affairs of the kingdom with such firmness, as greatly to augment its power and dignity. The Covenanters however withheld from him their support, and declared their adherence to Charles II., because of his solemn promise to maintain the "League and Covenant." After the expulsion of Charles from Scotland, by the army of Cromwell, the Protector prohibited the meeting of any General Assembly; but Presbyteries and Synods were allowed, and the church enjoyed a period of peace and tranquillity, beyond what it had ever before experienced. But on the death of Cromwell, Charles II. was by a series of intrigues restored to his throne, and soon made known his determination to violate all former promises, and at every hazard to restore prelacy throughout his kingdom.

Corrupt and wholly given to sensual pleasures, he drew around him and engaged in his service unprincipled and wicked men, who were too willing to carry out by the most oppressive and cruel measures his favourite policy. One of the first acts of his reign was the repeal of all laws which had been made in favour of the Presbyterian church and of civil liberty. This high-handed outrage against the Scottish nation was speedily sealed in the blood of some of their noblest citizens. The Marquis of Argyle was the first victim to regal tyranny and prelatic zeal. He had firmly resisted these encroachments on the liberties of the people, and he was hated by the king for the boldness with which he had formerly rebuked his wicked conduct.

He was therefore on some vain pretext tried and condemned and executed. James Guthrie, minister of Sterling, was the next martyr, dying serenely and cheerfully, and exclaiming almost prophetically with his last breath, "The Covenants, the Covenants shall yet be Scotland's reviving." Other distinguished ministers were cast into prison, or banished from the realm. When it was supposed that the spirit of the Presbyterian church was sufficiently humbled, preparation was made to accomplish the work of ruin, and four bishops were ordained at London to be set over the church of Scotland. Soon after, all meetings of Synods and Presbyteries were prohibited, until they should be authorized by the prelates, whose consecration had just taken place. An act was also passed, banishing from their homes and parishes all ministers who refused to conform to the prelatic order, and submit to be re-admitted to their several charges by the prelate within whose diocese they preached. It was supposed that few would refuse submission, and prefer to reverence their principles rather than their living. But the result proved far otherwise. On the last Sabbath in October, 1662, two hundred ministers took leave of their people, and in a few months four hundred pastors were ejected for non-conformity, leaving some of the fairest portions of Scotland waste.

Their places were soon filled with a crowd of worthless and ignorant men, who are declared, by Bishop Burnet, "to have been a disgrace to their orders and their sacred functions." The results of these changes can scarcely be imagined. The ejected ministers were compelled to leave their homes, around which their fondest affections centered, and the scenes of their long and earnest labours for the instruction and salvation of their people. In the depth of winter they turned away from all they held dear, because they would not perjure their souls, and sustain an order which they believed the Scripture did not allow. And their people, too, felt the change. They had long enjoyed the faithful ministrations of the word, and the simple preaching of the gospel. Then they were compelled to listen to men, for whom they could have no reverence, in whose piety they had no confidence, and whose knowledge of the Scriptures did not equal their own.

To attend the ministry of such men was impossible. A few aged ministers, however, were left where the oppressive act, by which so many suffered, had not reached. Hence, their churches were attended by crowds of people, often coming from great distances, to feast on the word of life. Some of the ejected pastors were also permitted to reside within their former parishes, and it became customary for many to collect at their houses, for family worship, where they had the privilege of hearing the word of God explained. Often, at such seasons, was it necessary for the company to betake themselves to the open air, so many were anxious to avail themselves of the opportunity of obtaining a taste of the good word of life. This was the beginning of those field meetings, or conventicles, against which such bitter persecution was soon after waged.

Nor was it long that this oppressed people could enjoy even the privilege of meeting for worship under the open sky. The army was pressed in to the aid of prelacy, and to assist in the destruction of religious liberty. New and oppressive acts were framed and enforced, a complete system of persecution matured, and a brutal soldiery set loose to accomplish its bloody work. The death of Charles II., in the year 1685, interrupted, for a brief while, the scenes of cruel butchery which were witnessed in Scotland, and closed up a life of treachery and ingratitude, of criminal pleasure, and open and shameless vice. The prelacy had been restored to power by men whose lives were blackened with crime, and by means from which every truly Christian mind, of whatever creed, recoils with horror.

The accession of James II. to the throne of England, only opened new scenes of trial to the church of Scotland. The king, though at first professing his desire to support the Protestant cause, was a bigoted papist, and discarding the advice of the wise and virtuous, gave himself up to the influence of Popish priests, and brought to his aid men whose names will be ever associated with vice and horrible inhumanity. In England, the brutal and infamous Jeffreys disgraced the office which should have been sacred to justice and right, by the most horrible acts of malice and outbursts of rage, against all who professed the principles of the Presbyterian church; while in Scotland, Claverhouse was making his name a terror, and spreading sorrow and death on every hand. Spies were sent forth to imitate the manners and language of the Covenanters; and thus to discover the hiding-places of those who were fleeing from persecution.

In this awful work, neither age nor sex was spared. At times all the inhabitants of a certain district would be driven together by an armed soldiery, and then compelled, either to renounce their religious faith, or pay the penalty of instant death. Again would the brutal Claverhouse collect the children from six to ten years of age, and order them to pray, for their last hour had come; then, while thus intimidated, he would offer them their lives, on the condition that they would discover where their parents and friends were concealed. Nor did he hesitate to imbrue his own hands in innocent blood, when his soldiers were reluctant to carry out his fiendish purposes. Many a scene of violence has been treasured up amid the traditions of Scotland, which show the terrible ordeal through which the church was called to pass, and

"Well, sir, well: the day of reckoning will come." p. 193.

the noble principles which were cherished by her sons, even in view of suffering and death.*

The following are but examples of the monstrous acts of oppression and cruelty which were then performed, for the purpose of forcing that people to conform to a religion, which they could not regard as in accordance with the teachings of God's word. The history of John Brown, of Lanarkshire, is familiar to many. For no crime but his piety and devotion to the Presbyterian church, he was shot down by Claverhouse, in the very presence of his wife and children.

The weeping and agonized widow, turning from the lifeless body of her husband, cried out to his murderer, "Well, sir, well; the day of reckoning will come." To which the brutal reply was, "To man I can answer for what I have done, and as to God, I will take him into mine own hand!"

A poor but respectable widow, who had sheltered a dying Covenanter, had her house pulled down, and she and her children were sent forth without a home. Her eldest son was taken before Claverhouse, who ordered him to be shot. When told to pull his bonnet over his face, he refused, and with his Bible in his hand, answered, "I can look

* "See Traditions of the Covenanters," in three volumes, published by the Board of Publication.

you in the face; I have done nothing of which I need be ashamed! But how will you look in that day when you shall be judged by what is written in this book?" So saying he fell, brutally murdered, and was buried in the moor. On the same day, an aged widow named Margaret Maclachlan, and Margaret Wilson, a girl of eighteen, were put to death for their religion. When they were offered their lives on condition of renouncing their faith, and attending Episcopal worship, they refused, and were accordingly sentenced to be drowned.

They were tied to stakes, fixed in the sand between high and low water mark. The tide first overwhelmed the aged sufferer, whose agony the youthful martyr beheld, while she yet possessed her calm serenity of mind. When asked what she thought of her fellow martyr, she replied, "What do I see but Christ in one of his members wrestling there? Think you that we are the sufferers? No; it is Christ in us; for he sends none a warfare on their own charges?"

When the cold waters began to rise around and over her own bosom, she prayed and sang praises, until the waves reached her lips. When life was almost extinct, she was released from her dreadful position, and asked if she would pray for the king.

"Dear Margaret," said one of the spectators, "say, God save the king." "God save him if he will," she replied, "for it is his salvation I desire." Major Windham, to whom her execution was committed, asked her if she would take the oath of abjuration. Firmly she answered, "I will not; I am one of Christ's disciples, let me go." She was then again plunged into the waters, and in a few moments entered her everlasting rest.

Such were the scenes of martyrdom witnessed in Scotland, during the brief reign of James II. In the year 1688 occurred the *Revolution*, by which the Popish tyrant was dethroned, and William and Mary called to rule over the English nation. Soon after the Presbyterian church was fully restored by law to all its ancient privileges, and this period of its sore and bitter trial passed away for ever.

A brief view of the formation of the Free General Assembly, and of the causes which led to it, is necessary to complete the history of the church of Scotland.

After the Revolution, by which a Protestant king was placed upon the throne of England, the Presbyterian form of government was established unalterably in Scotland, and the power of Parliament was exercised to support the authority of the church, and to sustain its ministry. When the union between the two nations was accomplished, it was made a condition of that act, "that no test or subscription should ever be imposed within the bounds of the Scotch church, contrary to their Presbyterian establishment."

Thus was formed a union between the civil and ecclesiastical powers, which, however much it might appear for the present peace and prosperity of the church, was to prove the source of immeasurable evil. Such a union can never be productive of good. It tends to corrupt the church, and to secularize its ministry. "The smile of Cæsar is the frown of Christ." And so it proved even in Scotland. It had ever been a principle with that people, that Christ was the supreme and only Head of the church, that the ministry was of his appointment, and that by his rule the church alone had the privilege of selecting its pastors and teachers. But during the reign of Queen Anne, an act was passed, giving to certain men the "right of patronage," or permission to nominate a pastor for a vacant parish. It is easy to see how soon corruption would follow such an act, and unworthy ministers be forced upon the people, often against their wishes, by patrons who cared little for their spiritual interest. And such was the result. Erskine, f r boldly denouncing the unrighteous law, was deposed, and in the year 1732, with a numerous body of ministers and their people, seceded from the established church, and formed the Associated Presbytery. But the great majority of the evangelical men were unwilling thus to break off from the ancient church, and continued within the bosom of the establishment, to struggle against the rising corruptions. With renewed zeal and earnestness they prayed and laboured for the truth and honour of God, and the conversion of souls. The divine blessing attended their efforts, and gracious revivals of religion were experienced in many portions of the country. But a departure from this apostolic spirit succeeded, as the church continued to feel the withering influence of an unhallowed union with the State. Ministers were selected and placed over churches against their expressed wishes, and men of ambition and worldliness, who knew little of the power and value of the gospel, were set as teachers and pastors over those for whose spiritual prosperity and growth they had no concern. Their preaching was a formal and heartless presentation of topics which could not satisfy the soul that was famishing for the bread of life. The great and distinctive feature of the gospel, as a dispensation of mercy, *solely through Christ*, was lost sight of, and worldly wisdom was introduced in its stead, and the people were left to hunger for the word of God. Those who sincerely loved the truth, mourned over these growing evils, and sought to arrest them.

In the year 1752, a second secession from the establishment was made, to afford relief to those churches that were suffering under the oppressions of the patronage system. The body thus formed assumed the name of the Relief Presbytery, of which the Rev. Thomas Boston and Thomas Gillespie were members. Still a large number of sound and evangelical men preferred to remain within the established church, as the most fitting and hopeful ground on which to resist the growing evils. Nor did they fail, whenever the opportunity occurred, to give their earnest testimony against the laws of patronage; or to rebuke publicly those ministers, who, under the influence of powerful but godless men, were forcing themselves upon churches that unanimously resisted their settlement. The subject of patronage was openly and often discussed, and the evils of a connection between the church and the State were topics which strongly attracted public attention. It became now a serious question, which, at length, agitated the whole church, whether there was any necessity for an interference of the State, with its own special duty, of providing for the people the means of religious instruction. On this subject the minds of even the most evangelical Christians were strangely in doubt. They had so long been accustomed to the unnatural alliance of civil and ecclesiastical power, as to be unable to perceive at once its impropriety. But the way was rapidly preparing for the exodus of Scotland from her long bondage. The evils of the right of patronage continued to press heavily upon the church.

Ministers were presented for installation over parishes to which they were wholly unacceptable, and on the refusal of Presbytery to sanction the act and accomplish the unrighteous deed, suits were instituted in civil courts, and damages awarded against the ministers acting in the case. Thus issue was made between the church and the State, and it remained to be seen whether the former would recede from its ancient doctrine, "that the Lord Jesus Christ, as the Head of the church, had given it power to decide its own matters of discipline, and to conduct all its internal arrangements." The result showed, as we shall see, that the spirit of the Reformation was not extinct, and that the Presbyterian church had still within its bosom those who were willing to stand up for the truth and the honour of God, at any sacrifice of personal ease and comfort.

The evils incident to an union of civil and ecclesiastical power, at length called loudly for decisive action on the part of the church of Scotland. It was evident that its purity and independence could only be maintained by disavowing the right of any one, to take from the people the choice of their own pastors. At the meeting of the General Assembly in May, 1842, petitions or "overtures" were sent from twelve Synods and twenty-four Presbyteries, praying for the abolition of patronage. A resolution was introduced, declaring it "to be a grievance that ought to be abolished;" and after a long and animated discussion was passed by a majority of sixty-nine. A "Claim of Rights, and Declaration against the encroachments of the civil power," was also drawn up, and decided by a majority of one hundred and thirty-one. In the discussion of these subjects, Dr. Chalmers bore a conspicuous part, and supported with all his great energies the rights of the church. These resolutions were presented to the Lord High Commissioner, who always sat in the General Assembly as the representative of the crown, with the request that they should be laid before her Majesty, the queen of England and Scotland.

The acts of the Assembly, though hailed with joy by all who truly loved the church, were met with fixed and determined opposition by the government. They savoured too much of that stern and indomitable love of freedom, and that spirit of republicanism, which had ever characterized the Presbyterian church. When the subject was introduced to the House of Commons, the claims of the church of Scotland were rejected by a large majority. It was henceforth apparent that a disruption must take place, and all needful preparations were made for it. Associations were formed, and funds raised to erect churches, and to support the ministry when aid should no longer be received from the government. A few days previous to the meeting of the General Assembly, a large number of ministers met at Edinburgh, and consulted respecting the final measures to be adopted, to maintain the purity and independence of the church. They resolved to prepare a protest, setting forth the encroachments which had been made by the State upon their religious rights, and giving a summary of the acts which were now compelling them to withdraw from the Establishment.

On the 18th of May, 1843, the General Assembly met at Edinburgh, in the church of St. Andrews. The Marquis of Bute, her Majesty's Commissioner, proceeded from the old Cathedral of St. Giles, and attended by the glitter of aristocratic pomp, and a long military and civic procession, and with the strains of martial music heralding his approach, entered the Assembly, and took his seat upon the throne. The meeting was then opened with prayer by the Moderator, Rev. Dr. Welsh. After a brief pause, as if weighing well the import of the words he was about to utter, he again, after a few explanatory sentences, proceeded to read the protest which had already been prepared. Then laying it on the table, he bowed to the Commissioner, and withdrew from the house, followed by all the evangelical party, among whom were those whose lives and works had shed the brightest lustre on that age of the church of Scotland. It was a solemn and momentous transaction. By that act they gave up their churches, and their manses, and forfeited their livings. Yet they deliberately and calmly went forth, led by His hand who had ever been to his people a wall of fire and an unfailing refuge. As they left the church, the dense crowd that filled the streets divided, as if by a single impulse, and through that vast sea of human beings those noble men passed on to the place provided for their meeting. Al-

The Exodus of the Free Church of Scotland. p. 203.

ready three thousand persons were gathered in the spacious hall, when the protesting ministers and elders entered. Dr. Welsh opened the meeting with prayer, amid the half suppressed emotions of the multitude, when many a manly face was bathed in tears. Dr. Chalmers was then chosen by acclamation, to be Moderator of the *first General Assembly of the Free Church of Scotland.* The 43d Psalm was sung, and prayer offered, and so the Assembly was regularly constituted. One of the first acts of this body was to prepare a "Deed of Demission," by which all connection with the government as an "established church" was renounced. On the 23d of May this was presented for signature. All other business was suspended. The roll was called, and in ranks of ten the members advanced and affixed their names to that momentous document, by which they gave up their homes, and all their worldly possessions, for the honour of *Christ, their King and Head.* Thus was the free church of Scotland enabled, by the grace of God, to effect its exodus from the bondage under which it had long groaned. It was a scene scarcely surpassed even amid the trials of the first Reformation. The present age of the world has never witnessed a nobler example of self-sacrifice for Christ and his cause. (See note F.)

With chastened feelings, yet with a calm and unshaken trust in God, the ministers of the Free church returned to their homes, and leaving the scenes of their former labours and joys, went forth as pilgrims and strangers to the toils and trials of pioneers. who were to lead the people forward in the new work assigned to them, and to bear with them the burden of forming new churches, and providing new means for the spiritual elevation of Scotland. And the result has proved, that He who called them forth has gone before them, and though calling them to endure afflictions, has given them abundant tokens of his presence and his love.

CHAPTER XVI.

THE PURITANS.

THE Reformation in England was carried forward by the influence of the king and his nobles, unlike the progress of the work in Scotland, where its principal actors were the *ministers and people.* Henry VIII., in his quarrel with the Pope, was made the instrument of effecting the first disruption between the churches of England and of Rome. Assuming for himself and his successors the title of "Supreme Head of the Church," he rendered it difficult to effect a reformation, further than what was deemed proper by the king and his counsellors, and thus made that great work dependent upon the caprice of monarchs, rather than upon the free and enlightened convictions of the people. After the death of Edward VI., Popery was restored, under the influence of the "Bloody Mary," and the cause of the Reformation was checked.

When Elizabeth came to the throne, the Protestant cause again obtained a partial triumph. But the Reformers soon learned that the queen, in her love of pomp and show, would oppose any thorough and radical change in the rites and forms of the Papal church. The most distinguished divines of that age desired a complete reformation, which should free the church from all the pageantry and corruptions that had crept in under the dominion of Rome. In this they were resisted by the queen, and compelled to mourn over the incompleteness of the work. Two parties thus sprang up in the ranks of English Protestants. The one, siding with the court, were satisfied to retain many of the external forms of Popery, slightly modified, and to introduce evangelical sentiments and doctrines, that they might (as they affirmed) the more easily induce the people to receive the more important changes which the Reformation had effected. The other party, from whom sprang the Puritans, affirmed that these relics of Popery only tended to perpetuate its influence, and to make it easy for the people to return thereto, should an opportunity offer. They desired, therefore, to leave as few traces of it as possible in the worship and order of the house of God. The court party continued to recognize the Papal church as a true church, though *somewhat corrupt;* while the Puritans regarded it as Antichrist and the Man of Sin.

The former declared that it was left to the civil magistrate to accommodate the government of the church to the condition of the State over which he ruled; while the latter held the Scriptures to be the only rule of practice and discipline, and desired to keep as near as possible to the model set forth in the word of God.

The queen, in her love of splendor and parade, gave all her influence and power to the party that sought to retain most of Papal superstition, and enacted severe and arbitrary laws to enforce uniformity thereto. A court was appointed, called the "High Commission," whose duty it was to investigate all offences against ecclesiastical laws. At the head of this court was placed Archbishop Parker, a bitter and violent enemy of the Puritans. Scenes of persecution now followed, which, while they disgraced the haughty and imperious prelates and their rulers, who thus sought to build up the interests of the church of England, only developed the more perfectly the Puritan spirit, and united those who cherished it. Scores of ministers were ejected from their livings, and churches were thus left without the means of religious instruction. The ruling party preferred that the people should be without the gospel and its ordinances, rather than that they should be administered by men who refused to conform to what they believed to be a relic of Popery.

It was not alone, however, against the vestments and ceremonies of the church that the Puritans contended. They questioned and denied the assumed authority of prelates as an order of the ministry superior to Presbyters, and objected to the discipline and government of the church, as thus constituted. They disapproved of the reading of the Apocryphal books in public worship; of confining the ministers to set forms of prayer; of keeping church festivals and saints' days, while the Sabbath was openly violated; and they declared the sign of the cross in baptism, and kneeling at the Lord's Supper, with many similar rites, to be both without Scriptural warrant, and an improper adherence to Papal forms and corruptions. For such causes they separated from the church of England. In November, 1572, fifteen ministers and eleven elders met and formed the First Presbytery of England, at Wandsworth, on the Thames. Thus the Puritans became fully organized, and though severe measures were enacted against them, they still continued to increase, so that before the death of Elizabeth their number was said to be 100,000. The accession of James I to the English throne only increased their sufferings, and many of them found refuge on the shores of the new world.

Charles I., on the death of his father, laboured, as we have already seen, to bring not only England, but Scotland and Ireland, under the power of his bishops. His chief counsellor was Archbishop Laud, a Papist at heart, under whom the most fearful severities were practised against those who refused to conform to the church of England. Yet the Puritans continued to increase. Parliament was itself brought under their power, and the Episcopacy was abolished, and an ordinance passed for the "calling *an assembly of godly and learned divines*, for the settling of the government and liturgy of the church, and cleansing its doctrines from false aspersions and interpretations."

This important ordinance is dated June 12, 1643. After declaring the present church government by archbishops, bishops, their chancellors, commissaries, deans and chapters, archdeacons, and other ecclesiastical officers depending upon the hierarchy, to be evil and justly offensive and burdensome to the kingdom, a great impediment to the Reformation and growth of religion, and very prejudicial to the state and government of this kingdom, and that the same shall be taken away; it is then added:

"Be it therefore ordained by the Lords and Commons, in this present Parliament assembled, that all and every the persons hereafter in this ordinance named, that is to say (here follow the names), and such other persons as shall be nominated and appointed by both houses of Parliament, &c., shall meet and assemble in the chapel called King Henry the Seventh's chapel, on the first day of July, 1643, and after the first meeting, being at least of the number of forty, shall from time to time sit, and be removed from place to place, and also that said assembly shall be dissolved, as by both houses of Parliament shall be directed." The ordinance then proceeds to define the duties of the assembly, viz.: to "confer and treat among themselves, of such matters and things touching and concerning the liturgy, discipline, and government of the church of England, or the clearing and vindicating the same from all false aspersions and misconstructions, as shall be proposed to them by both or either of the said houses of Parliament, and no other, and to deliver their opinion of or touching the matters aforesaid as shall be most agreeable to the word of God, to both or either of the said houses, from time to time, in such manner and sort, as by both or either of the said houses of Parliament shall be required, and the same not to divulge by printing, writing, or otherwise, without the consent of both or either house of Parliament."

The Westminster Assembly of divines held their first meeting on the first of July, 1643, and continued its sessions for five years and seven months. It was composed, by order of Parliament, of ten lords, twenty commoners, and one hundred and twenty-one ministers, among whom were some of the most eminent and learned men of the age. Of this number four bishops were named, one of whom was present at the opening, and another excused himself from attendance on the ground of necessary duty.

Several Episcopalians beside were appointed, although most of them withdrew, because the Assembly did not enjoy the approbation of the king. It was the wish of the Parliament to act with fairness and impartiality, and to have all opinions, especially on church government, represented.

The two prominent parties in the Assembly, were those who held views favourable to Presbyterianism, and those who regarded each church as independent of all others, and who rejected the idea of responsibility or subordination to higher courts. These were called Independents, and they were well and ably represented in the Assembly.

Four Scottish divines were also present, and took part throughout in the deliberations of this venerable body.

For the regular and orderly conduct of business, the whole Assembly was divided into three equal committees; the divines according to the order in which their names stood in the ordinance, and the Lords and Commons into their corresponding divisions, also according to their order. Each committee chose its own chairman, who presided in its special deliberations, after which the subjects specially brought before them were discussed in the full Assembly. (See note G.)

The attention of the Assembly was first directed to a careful review of the doctrines of the church of England; but, at the request of Parliament, this subject was laid aside after a brief discussion, in order to prepare a directory for worship, and a form of government and discipline. After keeping a solemn fast, and earnestly imploring the divine guidance and blessing, they commenced their deliberations. Committees were appointed to prepare subjects for public discussion, and after their reports were made, the Assembly engaged in arguments thereon, until all the members had opportunity to express their opinions, and then the question was decided by vote. On many subjects of church order and discipline there was often a keen and protracted discussion, yet, by the final decision of the Assembly, the Presbyterial form of government was adopted, and declared by an act of Parliament to be "lawful and agreeable to the word of God." The Confession of Faith was then framed, and the Scriptural proof of each article annexed thereto, after which the Larger and Shorter Catechisms were drawn up, for the instruction of children, and those comparatively ignorant of religious truth. These works contain a summary of Christian doctrine, presenting, in a simple and concise manner, all the important truths which are taught in the word of God. When they were finished, all the chief matters for which the Assembly had been called together were completed, and that body was finally dissolved on the 22d of February, 1649. This period in the history of England was full of momentous events. Prelacy had been abolished, and king Charles I. had suffered death at the hands of men who saw no hope of liberty but in his execution. Cromwell obtained the supremacy, and governed the nation with a firmness and decision that gained for England the respect of all nations. The Puritans, though their power was brief, yet were enabled to accomplish a reformation, whose influence is still felt over the world.

Those clear and consistent outlines of Christian truth, which they prepared during the long deliberations of the Westminster Assembly, are the great standards of our church, every one of which is built upon and supported by the word of God. And thousands of minds have thereby been fitted to withstand the assaults of error, and to hold fast the faith once delivered to the saints.

Amid all the convocations of the church, in modern times, not one has been of such importance in its influence as that of which we have spoken. No outline of Christian doctrine embodies more of Scriptural truth, adapted to the minds of children, than the Shorter Catechism, which, beginning with just ideas of God, leads us on through all that the Scriptures principally teach, both concerning him and the duties he requires of us. It was composed by men who were deeply read in the word of God, and whose hearts sincerely received "the truth in the love of it;" and its influence, when properly taught, is to establish the mind firmly in the great doctrines of the gospel.

The standards of doctrine and discipline established by the Westminster Assembly, were cordially received by the church of Scotland, as embodying the great principles for which the Reformers contended, and as being wholly in accordance with the instructions of the Scriptures. Nor did England cease to feel their influence even when it had restored prelacy to power. The heart of the nation still felt the impulse which those truths had communicated to it. The ablest and best bishops and clergy of the church, who bore a part in the Revolution which gave Protestantism and liberty to the people, received, in their youth, the instruction of Presbyterian professors in the universities, and there learned to love those doctrines and principles, the development of which made England free, and afterward gave to America the pure gospel and the blessings of liberty.

CHAPTER XVII.

THE PRESBYTERIAN CHURCH IN IRELAND.

THE early Christians of Ireland have already been noticed as witnesses for the truth, who for centuries retained in their churches the faith and discipline of the apostolic age. For a thousand years religion flourished under the auspices of a church, resembling in its essential features the liberal and republican form of government now called Presbyterian. In the year 1172, Henry II. of England established the Roman church in the city of Dublin, where, to the present day, the people are more deeply attached to the Papal faith than in any other portion of Ireland. Under the new influences thus brought to bear upon that people, the original inhabitants gradually disappeared from the territory around Dublin, and the ancient church decreased in popularity and power, until only one representative of its former strength and order remained at Armagh, which united with the Reformed church in the year 1626. The primitive church was never therefore wholly extinguished.

Under the reign of James I., inducements were held out to the Protestant citizens to emigrate thither, and thus to reintroduce the faith of the Reformed churches to Ireland. Colonies of both Scotch and English were soon planted there. The former earnestly desired the services and instruction of Presbyterian ministers, but were compelled at first to forego their wishes in the prevalence of Episcopacy, under the intolerance of the reigning monarch.

In 1613, the Rev. Edward Bryce, formerly minister in Stirlingshire, emigrated to Ireland, and settled in Broad Island, in the county of Antrim. He was soon followed by others of the same faith, who, though licensed to preach by an Episcopal bishop, maintained the Presbyterian order and worship, greatly to the dissatisfaction of Bishop Ecklin, who suspended six of their number. Under the influence of Archbishop Laud, now in power, such sore and grievous persecution was stirred up against them, that in the year 1636, one hundred and forty, including several ministers, embarked at Carrick-fergus for America; hoping to find here that liberty and peace which was denied them at home. But adverse winds compelled them to return, and the ministers escaped to Scotland. A system of tyranny and cruel persecution was now commenced against them, which continued in some form or other until the dreadful massacre, in which thousands of Protestants, both of the English and Scotch churches, shared alike the brutal and fiendish malice of the Romish church. This memorable event occurred October 23d, 1641.

On the 10th of June, 1642, five ministers and four elders from the church of Scotland organized the Presbyterian church of Ireland, in the city of Carrick-fergus. Commencing as it did, within a few months after the enactment of those horrid butcheries, the recital of which produces even now a shudder, the church enjoyed the evidence of the favour of its great Head, and under his smiles flourished and strengthened.

The following statements will serve to present a general outline of the present state of Presbyterianism in Ireland. There are now eight distinct ecclesiastical bodies, of which three are heterodox.

The first and most important is the General Assembly of the Presbyterian church. This is Scotch in its origin, having been formed by ministers of the Kirk of Scotland. It is composed of the General Synod of Ulster, and the Synod of the Secession church, which in 1840 united in one body. It now numbers five Synods, thirty-six Presbyteries, four hundred and thirty-nine congregations, and five hundred and thirty-three ministers. It is a sound and able body, nobly engaged in the work of missions, at home and abroad, and earnestly contending for the truth.

It has sent out missionaries to the Jews in Damascus, and to those who are dispersed throughout Germany. It has also its faithful representatives in Hindostan, in the British colonies of America, in Africa and Australia. It is also actually engaged at home in disseminating the truths of the gospel among Roman Catholics. Since the commencement of its domestic missionary work in 1823, it has added more than fifty churches to its numbers, whose members are mostly converted Romanists.

It is also doing much for the cause of a liberal and Christian education, having two flourishing colleges under its control, one of which (the Assembly's College at Belfast) is devoted mainly to the work of theological instruction. The other institution is at Londonderry, ever memorable in the history of Irish Protestantism, as the scene of some of its earliest labours and sorest trials.

The churches in connection with the General Assembly are large and influential, their ministers occupy the most important positions in society, and rank with the nobility.

The Synod of Munster, the Presbytery of Antrim, and the Remonstrant Synod, were formed severally in 1660, 1727, and 1830. They hold to errors in doctrine for which they withdrew from the church, and have no connection with it.

The other Presbyterian bodies are, the Reformed Presbyterian, consisting of five Presbyteries, and twenty-seven ministers; the Eastern Reformed Presbyterian Synod, having two Presbyteries and eight ministers; the Associate Presbytery, and the Presbytery of Munster, which is in correspondence with the General Assembly in Ireland.

With the exception of the three small bodies noticed above, these all hold to the order and doctrines of the Reformed churches of the continent and of Scotland. From them came many of the founders of the American church, who, uniting with the members of the same faith from Scotland, and England, and France, and Switzerland, established on the shores of the New World the institutions for which their fathers had laboured, and on whose behalf many had suffered persecution and affliction, and the loss of all things.

CHAPTER XVIII.

THE AMERICAN PRESBYTERIAN CHURCH, FROM ITS FOUNDATION TO THE WAR OF THE REVOLUTION.

DURING those scenes of persecution and trial of which we have spoken, and through which the church passed, while freeing herself from the corruptions of the Papacy, God was preparing a refuge for his people, upon the shores of the New World.

Early in the seventeenth century the colonization of this country began, and the institutions of the Christian religion were established here. In 1620 there were members of the Reformed church of Holland in New Amsterdam, now New York; and six years after a small church was built for their use. This was connected with, and dependent upon, the churches of Holland, whose Presbyterial constitution has already been noticed.

In the winter of 1620 the Pilgrim Fathers of New England landed at Plymouth, after having first found refuge from persecution in Holland, where they had opportunity to become acquainted with the development of republican principles and true liberty, both in the church and the State. From this time the tide of emigration rapidly set towards the western world, to which the oppressed and persecuted disciples of Christ looked for a refuge and a home. While the first colony of English Puritans were Independents, or Congregationalists, many who followed them, and especially those who settled in Connecticut and New Hampshire, were Presbyterians, who, while they fell in with the form of church organization which they found already established, preferred and sought to introduce, as far as possible, the elements of Presbyterian discipline into their churches. In the year 1648, a Convention, or Synod, was held at Cambridge, at which articles of discipline were adopted, which, in many important features, resemble those of the Presbyterian church. (See Note J.) The officers of the church are set forth as consisting of pastors, or bishops, ruling elders, and deacons; and Synods are described as "having power to determine controversies of faith and cases of conscience, to bear witness against maladministration and corruption in doctrine or manners in any particular church, and to give directions for the reformation thereof."

The Synod which met at Saybrook, in 1708,

prepared a "Platform" still more like the form of government adopted by the churches of Scotland, Holland, Geneva, and France. Thus the influence of Presbyterian principles pervaded the churches of New England to a very great extent. Even in many of the Independent congregations, ruling elders formed an essential part of their organization; and their most distinguised ministers testified to an earnest wish for the preservation of this office in the church.

It was the dying regret of Mr. Wilson, one of the earliest ministers of Boston, that among the sins of the people was "opposition to the elders, and a want of subjection to the authority of Synods, without which the churches cannot long subsist."

So, also, Eliot declared, "there were specially two things which he was loth to see, and yet feared he saw falling in the churches of New England; one was a thorough establishment of ruling elders, and the other a frequent repetition of needful Synods."

Such were the sentiments of thousands who early emigrated to America, and who were scattered over the eastern colonies, and portions of what now form the Middle States. Besides these, there were large numbers of refugees from France, who, after the revocation of the "Edict of Nantes," sought an asylum from oppression and persecution, amid the scenes of the New World.

From Scotland, also, there came many of her hardy and virtuous sons to swell the vast army now preparing to take its proper position among the American churches, on the side of truth, and under the banner of the Prince of Peace, while from Piedmont a band of persecuted Waldenses came, to find refuge in the New World, and to assist in the establishment of the church upon its fair and fertile shores. Such were the materials of which the Presbyterian church in America was formed. In that vast crowd of emigrants, who, before the close of the seventeenth century, were to be found in New England, and in what are now the Middle and Southern States, were thousands of men, who were Calvinists in doctrine, and whose views of church order coincided with those held in Scotland, and among the Puritans of England. Hence, even in New England, where Independent or Congregational influences most prevailed, the people were familiar with the government of the church by elders, and with the existence of Synods, whose power was little inferior to that of our own higher church-courts.

About the year 1690, Francis Makemie, from

the north of Ireland, and John Hampton, from Scotland, who were labouring as missionaries on behalf of a society in London, succeeded in organizing churches after the Scottish model in the eastern part of Maryland. A company of Scotch emigrants also were organized as a church at the same time, who came in a body to this country, with their pastor, Rev. Nathaniel Taylor, and settled in Upper Marlborough.

The churches of Snowhill, Rehoboth, Monokin, and Wicomico were formed by Mr. Makemie, whose name and memory are still cherished, as an able and devoted servant and minister of Christ.

In 1698, the first Presbyterian church of Philadelphia was formed by a number of English, Welsh, and French Protestants, who united under the pastoral care of Rev. Mr. Andrews of Boston. Early in the last century, churches were organized in various parts of Pennsylvania, New Jersey, Delaware, South Carolina, and New York, and thus the foundations were laid, of those institutions which under God, have been powerful for the extension of the truths of the gospel, and for the promotion of civil and religious liberty throughout our land.

The churches which had been gathered under the labours of Makemie, and other ministers, chiefly from Scotland and Ireland, were, in the year 1704, organized into the Presbytery of Philadelphia. The original members of that body were Rev. Messrs. Makemie, Andrews, McNish, Wilson, Taylor, and Davis. With the exception of Mr. Andrews, it is supposed that they were ordained by Presbyters in Scotland or Ireland. The first ordination performed by them, after their organization, was that of Mr. John Boyd, who was pastor of a church in Freehold, New Jersey.

In 1716, the number of ministers having increased to twenty-five, three new Presbyteries were created, viz.: New Castle, Snowhill, and Long Island, which together constituted the Synod of Philadelphia. Thus was the American branch of the Presbyterian church constituted, and from this time its growth was rapid and sure. Its numbers and strength were greatly augmented by accessions from the churches of Scotland, France, Holland and Switzerland, which, from the times of the Reformation, had adopted the Presbyterian faith and order.

Owing to the liberal and enlightened policy pursued towards all denominations by the Quakers of Pennsylvania, and the toleration required under the charter of Maryland, these colonies were the favoured resort for Presbyterians, who were fleeing from the persecutions waged against them in England and Scotland. Here they found an asylum; here their first churches were gathered, and here they began to enjoy the benefit of those principles for which they had suffered. Yet even on the shores of the New World they were not wholly free from persecution, and were compelled often to feel the power of that hierarchy from which they had sought to escape.

In the year 1707, Messrs. Makemie and Hampton, in the prosecution of their missionary work, visited New York, where a number of French Calvinists and other Presbyterians, having no house of worship, had been in the habit of meeting at private houses every Sabbath. On this occasion permission was obtained to occupy the Dutch church, by Mr. Makemie, on the next Lord's day. This the Governor prohibited, and, accordingly, Mr. Makemie preached in a private house, while Mr. Hampton officiated at Newtown, Long Island. For this act both of these ministers were arrested and imprisoned for six weeks and four days, when they were admitted to bail. Against Mr. Hampton no indictment was found, and Mr. Makemie, though acquitted upon his trial, was not released until he had paid a sum exceeding two hundred dollars.

Five years before this act, the same Governor, Lord Cornbury, had fixed his residence at Jamaica, Long Island, during the fatal prevalence of fever in New York. Here the people had erected a neat Presbyterian church, and a house for their pastor. In the second service upon the Sabbath, as the people entered their church, they found the pulpit occupied by an Episcopal minister, and the principal seats by the Governor and his dependants, nor were they permitted again for many years to worship in that building which they had themselves erected. As if to crown this act of oppression, the parsonage, which had been generously offered to the Governor for his use, was, on his return to the city, left in possession of the Episcopal missionary, by whom and his successor it continued to be occupied for twenty-five years, and the glebe which had been given for the support of the gospel, was seized by the sheriff, and leased out for the maintenance of Episcopal worship. To many such acts of oppression were the ministers and members of the Presbyterian church compelled to submit, in their early efforts to introduce their principles and order into the colony of New York under the English rule.

In Virginia, also, they were met with more serious difficulties. For an hundred years after the first settlement of that colony, the most severe and arbitrary laws were enforced against all who differed from the Established Church of England. Attendance on meetings of non-conformists was punished by fines; and no dissenter might preach either in public or private, under the penalty of banishment from the colony. Yet against the obstacles thus thrown in its way, the church advanced in strength and numbers. Its ministers were faithful and able men, who loved the truth, and earnestly desired the upbuilding of the kingdom of Christ, and they laboured zealously and perseveringly to lay the foundations of the church upon the shores of the Western world. And, as we shall see, the great Head of the church smiled upon their labours, and gave them abundant tokens of his love and favour.

Soon after the organization of the Synod of Philadelphia, it became apparent that entire harmony of opinion, on all subjects relating to the interests of the church, could not be readily secured. One class of ministers were in favour of strict Presbyterianism, a rigid adherence to its order and discipline, and high attainments in learning, in all who desired to be admitted to the ministry. Another party undervalued the order and discipline of the church, human knowledge, and theological science, and laid great stress on the possession of ardent piety, rather than attainments in literature, in candidates for the work of preaching the gospel In the year 1728 an overture was presented to Synod from the Presbytery of New Castle, respecting the subscription by ministers to the Westminster Confession of Faith. After it was read, the consideration of it was postponed until the next meeting, to give time for deliberation and opportunity for every member of Synod to be present at the discussion of the subject.

Accordingly, in the year 1729, the Adopting Act was passed, by which the Westminster Confession of Faith and Catechisms were received as the standards of doctrine and order in the American branch of the Presbyterian church. But though thus adopted, they did not receive the cordial assent of the whole body; so that misunderstandings and unhappy prejudices increased, and parties were formed, between which alienation of feeling at length grew into open rupture.

During the year 1739, Whitefield visited America for the second time, and his preaching was followed by a most wonderful outpouring of the Spirit of God, and multitudes were made the subjects of renewing grace. This great awakening proved the occasion of a still wider breach in the church.

A portion of its ministers looking chiefly at certain irregularities, which were mingled with the work of grace, too readily pronounced the whole a delusion, while others were warmly in favour of Whitefield, and if they did not approve of all his measures, heartily rejoiced in the good which he accomplished. The two parties, to which were given the names of "Old" and "New Side," were now fully separated. Both contained good men, who acted, as they conscientiously believed, for the best interests of the church, and the glory of its great Head.

At length the rupture was complete, and the Synod of New York was formed, comprising within its limits those who had been usually known as "New Side" men. Among the distinguished ministers of that period, were the Rev. William Tennent and his four sons, Presidents Dickinson, Burr, Edwards and Davies, who were called New Side men, and Messrs. Thompson, Cross, and Dr. Allison, who were numbered with the other party. They were men in whom was the spirit of true piety, and an ardent love for the church. During the period of their separation, both Synods engaged earnestly in missionary enterprises, seeking to form new congregations, wherever the way was prepared. They also engaged zealously in efforts to promote the cause of education. The college at Princeton was mainly indebted to them for its existence and endowment. In consequence of a petition from the trustees, Messrs. Gilbert Tennent and Samuel Davies visited England and Scotland, and secured sufficient funds to erect a convenient college building, and to lay a foundation for a fund to support necessary instructors.

In the year 1758, seventeen years after the division, the two Synods were again united, under the name of the Synod of New York and Philadelphia. The members had grown tired of controversy; they felt that there was no good ground for separation, and by mutual concessions were again ready to unite in a common bond of Christian communion. Negotiations for such a union had been in progress for several years, and committees of conference had met and compared views on various matters of interest and importance, respecting the order and purity of the church. The articles of agreement which had been proposed were at length unanimously adopted, by both the Synods meeting for the purpose in Philadelphia.

From this memorable period they moved on harmoniously and prosperously, rapidly increasing in numbers and strength, and enlarging on every hand the borders of the church. The number of ministers had increased to nearly one hundred, among whom were men distinguished both for their piety and their learning, whose names still shed a lustre upon the annals of our church and the nation, and who, while they zealously sought the upbuilding of the Redeemer's kingdom, loved their country, and upheld her rights and liberties when invaded by tyranny and oppression.

When the union between the Synods of Philadelphia and New York had been happily accomplished, the church renewed its efforts to supply the destitute with the means of grace, and with proper facilities for education.

The field occupied by the Synod was extensive, and rapidly filling with population. To keep pace with the demand for ministers and churches required the utmost diligence and labour. Funds were raised and appropriated for missions among the Indians, and ministers were sent out to preach among the southern and western provinces, as Providence opened a way before them. Thus the bounds of the church were gradually extended.

In Virginia, where the early Presbyterians met with opposition from the intolerance of the Established church, congregations had been gathered, and a Presbytery formed, under whose direction the work of missions was now carried forward with increased activity. From North and South Carolina, and Georgia, petitions were received for ministerial supplies, in answer to which commissioners were appointed to visit those portions of the country, and "form societies, ordain elders, administer sealing ordinances, instruct the people in discipline, and finally direct them in their conduct, particularly in what manner they should proceed to obtain the stated ministry." To make more ample and permanent provision for the work of home missions, it was ordered by Synod that there should be an annual collection taken up in every congregation; that every Presbytery should appoint a treasurer to receive and transmit the moneys thus obtained; that the Synod should appoint a general treasurer, to whom all these collections should be sent; and that every year a full account of all receipts and disbursements should be printed, and sent down among the churches. This arrangement was made in the year 1767, and is a witness to the fidelity with which the fathers of the American church sought to fulfil their duties to the destitute population of this land.

With equal earnestness they endeavoured to advance the cause of education, especially in preparing poor and pious young men for the ministry, and it was also enjoined on all congregations "to pay a special regard to the good education of children, as being intimately connected with the interests of religion and morality; that they be particularly careful to procure able and virtuous teachers; that they make the erection of schools a part of their congregational business, and endeavour to induce the people to support them by their contributions, being not only the most effectual, but in the end the cheapest way of supporting them."

It was also enjoined on the sessions of churches "to visit the schools at least once in three months, to inquire into the conduct of the master and the improvement of the children, and to observe particularly his care to instruct them at least one day in the week in the principles of religion." Thus were the foundations of the Presbyterian church laid, and her borders extended over this land, soon to become the home of freedom and the asylum of the oppressed.

In the year 1776 the United States became a separate nation, and the war of the Revolution commenced. In that conflict the Presbyterian church threw its whole influence in favour of liberty. Dr. Witherspoon, then President of the College of New Jersey, was appointed a representative of that State to the Continental Congress at Philadelphia, and was one of the Signers of the Declaration of Independence, taking also an active part in the deliberations of the body of which he was a member, thus showing himself to be not only an eminent theologian, but a sound civilian, and a sincere and ardent patriot. The Synod also sent forth repeated counsels to the churches under its care, appointed days of fasting when certain crises in the Revolution seemed to call for special prayer to God, and endeavoured, by every means in their power, to strengthen the hands of those who were fighting in what they felt to be a righteous cause. When peace was finally restored, and the nation emerged from that period of gloom and sore trial in which it had been plunged, the Synod again issued a pastoral letter to the churches, recounting the signal mercies of God, which had been manifested in giving liberty to the people, and calling upon them devoutly to acknowledge, and gratefully to remember, his distinguishing goodness.

From this time the church continued to gain rapidly in strength and influence. Its missionary enterprises, which had been greatly embarrassed during the war, were again resumed, and carried forward with abundant tokens of the divine approval and blessing. Congregations which had been broken up were revived; ministerial intercourse, which had been suspended, was again enjoyed, and the church commenced a new career of activity and usefulness

CHAPTER XIX.

THE AMERICAN PRESBYTERIAN CHURCH, FROM THE REVOLUTION TO THE PRESENT TIME.

THE close of the war of the Revolution, and the establishment of American independence, made a reorganization of the church necessary. That great struggle, although it had in many points proved disastrous to its immediate interests, had yet received the hearty co-operation of its ministers.

Dr. Witherspoon had been chosen to represent the State of New Jersey in the Continental Congress, and his name is affixed to the Declaration of Independence, of whose principles he was a firm supporter, while the whole body of the ministry had, from the commencement of the struggle, taken a deep interest in behalf of the rights and liberties of the colonies.

When peace was declared, the Synod addressed a pastoral letter to their congregations, congratulating them on the general and almost universal attachment of the Presbyterian body to the cause of liberty, and the rights of mankind. "This," say they, "has been visible in their conduct, and has been confessed by the complaints and resentment of the common enemy. Such a circumstance ought not only to afford us satisfaction on the review, but to increase our gratitude to God for the happy issue of the war. Had it been unsuccessful, we must have drunk deeply of the cup of suffering. Our burnt and wasted churches, and our plundered dwellings, in such places as fell under the power of our adversaries, are but an earnest of what we must have suffered had they finally prevailed. The Synod, therefore, request you to render thanks to Almighty God, for all his mercies, spiritual and temporal, and in a particular manner for establishing the independence of the United States of America. He is the supreme Disposer, and to him belong the glory, the victory, and the majesty."

Until this period, since the reunion of the Synod of New York and Philadelphia, the whole business of the church had been devolved upon that one body. In the large increase which had taken place, it had become evident that there must be a new arrangement entered into, by which the interests of the several portions of the country might be better subserved. Accordingly, in the year 1786, it was resolved to revise the public standards of the church, and to establish three or more Synods, out of which a General Assembly should be formed. The committee to whom this duty was assigned consisted of Rev. Dr. Witherspoon, Dr. Rodgers, Dr. Robert Smith, and others, who spent several months in accomplishing these important labours.

In May 1788, the revision of the articles of faith and discipline was completed, and it was resolved to erect four Synods, viz: the Synod of New York and New Jersey, Philadelphia, Virginia, and of the Carolinas. These were to be united in a General Assembly, after the model of the Church of Scotland. The Westminster Confession of Faith, with the alteration of those articles which favoured the establishment of the institutions of religion in connection with the civil power, was adopted by the Presbyteries to whom it was submitted, after a full and free discussion.

The Synod which met in 1788 to make the final arrangement, formally ratified and adopted the Constitution of the Presbyterian church, the Directory for Worship, and the Standards of Doctrine, and then resolved,

"That the first meeting of the General Assembly to be constituted out of the four Synods, be held, and it is hereby appointed to be held, on the third Thursday of May, 1789, in the second Presbyterian church in the city of Philadelphia, at 11 o'clock, A. M., and that Dr. Witherspoon, or in the case of his absence Dr. Rodgers, open the General Assembly with a sermon, and preside until a moderator be chosen."

The time and places of meeting for the new Synods were then appointed, after which the Synod of New York and Philadelphia was dissolved, and the session concluded with prayer. Thus was closed the history of that large and venerable body, under whose care and labours the Presbyterian Church had grown and strengthened, and enjoyed rich and abundant tokens of the divine presence and blessing. More than ninety years had passed since its first ministers had been sent forth from Scotland, to establish here those religious institutions for which that people had long and earnestly contended. And although in that period the church had suffered from division, and had felt the fearful and blighting influences of a protracted war, yet it had grown from a few feeble and scattered congregations to four hundred and twenty churches, with one hundred and seventy-seven ministers, forming sixteen Presbyteries. A new era had now dawned upon it.

The political institutions of the country had experienced a great and important change, and it was proper the church should prepare herself for more enlarged and systematic efforts to meet the demands which were now made for the extension of her borders, and the supply of new fields of labour with the ministry of reconciliation and the means of grace.

In the month of May, 1789, the first General Assembly of the Presbyterian church, in the United States, met in Philadelphia. Two months before, the Federal Government of the nation had been fully organized, by the adoption of the Constitution, and the inauguration of George Washington as President of the new republic, at the city of New York. The same year, therefore, that saw the beginning of our national organization, witnessed, also, the completion of the Presbyterian system in America, as it had long existed in Scotland, and between which and the republican institutions of the country there was a marked similarity.

According to previous arrangement, Dr. Witherspoon preached the opening sermon of the Assembly. This able and distinguished divine was a native of Scotland, and a lineal descendant of John Knox, through his daughter, the wife of John Welsh, of whom mention has been made in connection with the early struggles of the Scottish church. At the urgent solicitation of the friends of Princeton college, he removed to this country, and assumed the management of that venerable institution, over which he presided until his death, which occurred in November, 1794.

Connected as he had been with the American church for a period of twenty years, and identified with her highest interests, to the promotion of which he had given the full strength of his genius, it was natural that the eyes of his brethren in the ministry should look to him as the proper person to preside at the opening of the highest court of the church, and to take a prominent part in the services of that occasion.

After the organization of the Assembly, the Rev. Dr. Rodgers, of New York, was chosen the first Moderator. This venerable divine was converted under the preaching of Whitefield, and commenced his labours, as a licentiate, in the colony of Virginia, in connection with Rev. Mr. Davies. Having been forbidden by the authorities to continue preaching within "the dominion," he passed into Maryland, and thence returned to Pennsylvania, where he found four calls awaiting his decision. One of them was from St. Georges, in the colony of Delaware, and although that congregation was the smallest and feeblest of the four churches that solicited his labours, he accepted the invitation, was ordained in March, 1749, by the Presbytery of New Castle, and continued his labours there until May, 1765, when he was removed to take charge of the Presbyterian church in the city of New York. Here he threw the whole weight of his energy and influence in behalf of the Presbyterian cause, and was most successful in his efforts for its promotion and prosperity. In the war of the Revolution, Dr. Rodgers took an earnest and decided stand in favour of American Independence. Early in the struggle he removed his family from the city to a place of retirement. When Washington reached New York, Dr. Rodgers waited upon him to pay his respects, and was received by him with marked attention. When about to retire, the General followed him to the door, and observed that "his name had been mentioned to him while in Philadelphia, as one whose fidelity to the interests and liberty of the country might be relied on, and who might be capable of giving him important information;" and added, "May I take the liberty, sir, to apply to you whenever circumstances may render it desirable?"

The Doctor assured him of his readiness to render him any assistance in his power, and in several instances was enabled to do so, as was afterwards shown by letters and papers found after his death.

On his return to the city, at the close of the war, the two churches in which he ministered, viz., the Wall street and the Brick church, had been used by the British soldiers; the former as a barracks, and the latter as a hospital. While these were repairing, the congregation, by the kind offer of Trinity church, was permitted to worship in the two chapels of St. George's and St. Paul's. When the standards of the church were to be revised, and changes made in the Synod, which had hitherto been the highest ecclesiastical court, Dr. Rodgers took an active part in the work, and, as we have already seen, was chosen to be the Moderator of the First General Assembly of the Presbyterian church in the United States. The arrangement of the church was now completed. Of the venerable men who composed that first Assembly, all have passed away, but the foundations which they laid were strong and massive, and yet remain in all their strength and beauty. Sixty-five years have passed since that memorable era, during which the church has moved on with amazing prosperity and success, rapidly increasing in numbers and strength, and while not without trials and divisions, has enjoyed marked and special evidences of the smile and favour of God.

The General Assembly, at its first meeting, had under its care less than two hundred ministers, and a large number of vacant congregations. To supply the growing wants of the country for spiritual instruction was one of its first efforts. A plan of missionary operations was at once adopted, for the carrying out of which the Presbyteries were required to transmit their funds to the Assembly. In the year 1802, a more complete system was commenced, by which the work was committed to a standing committee on missions, and in 1828 the plan was perfected by constituting a Board of Missions, who, being responsible to the Assembly, were authorized to take charge of the work of supplying destitute regions with the ordinances of the sanctuary. The necessity of providing means for educating young men for the ministry, early enlisted the attention of the church.

Princeton college, as has already been noticed, was one of the noble results of the efforts made in that direction. In the year 1812, a theological seminary was established at the same place; and similar institutions were founded in other sections of the country, as the demand for the ministry in creased.

In the early part of the present century it was deemed advisable, for the purpose of meeting the wants of new and sparsely settled districts, where the inhabitants were divided in their sentiments respecting the Congregational and Presbyterian forms of church government, and were yet unable to sustain two separate churches, to allow of an organization which might harmonize both opinions, and thus permit them, without giving up their own views, to enjoy the ordinances of the gospel. This "Plan of Union," although it never became fully a law, because never submitted regularly to the Presbyteries, was permitted to operate for more than thirty years.

But although its original design was good, it came at length to be attended with evils on which good men looked with pain and regret. It was the means of introducing within the bounds of the church many congregations and ministers, who had little sympathy for its order, or even for its doctrines, and while professedly connected with it, were throwing their influence against its institutions and its principles. The evils which were thus spreading called for some decisive action. But on the nature of the action required, there was unhappily a wide difference of opinion. In the yea. 1837 it was resolved, by the General Assembly, to abrogate the "Plan of Union," and to declare those Synods and Presbyteries, where churches were framed after that plan, no longer a part of the Presbyterian church. These acts, though they were proposed and sustained by men whose praise was in all the churches, were warmly opposed by others, who regarded them as unconstitutional and oppressive, and who withdrew from the Assembly in the succeeding year and formed a separate organization. It was not possible for a division like this to take place without intense excitements and frequent and unhappy collisions. On either side were noble men, acting from pure motives, from strong convictions of duty, and from earnest desires to promote the peace and purity of the church.

They stood in defence of the order of the house of God, though brought thereby into separation from many whom they had long known and loved as brethren.

For thirty years the two bodies, known by way of distinction as Old and New School, acted independently. Yet, as time passed on, and ministers and churches of both sides grew up together, forgetting past differences in their efforts to spread the truth and to save souls, the question often forced itself upon the minds of many who had strong convictions in respect to the questions on which the division had been made, whether the time was not approaching when a reunion was desirable? Both churches held to the same Confession of Faith and Form of Government, and on many of the questions, especially in regard to Church Polity, there was substantial agreement. The great work of extending the church at home and abroad seemed also especially to demand a union of all who held the Presbyterian Faith and Order. These questions assumed a definite and practical shape during the meeting of the two Assemblies at St. Louis in the year 1865, when a committee was appointed from both bodies to confer together and arrange a plan of reunion, to be submitted to the next Assemblies. It was not until the meeting at New York, in 1869, that the conditions of union were perfected. So full and substantial was the accord at this time that both Assemblies adjourned to meet at Pittsburg in the autumn of the same year, at which time the Presbyteries to whom the plan was submitted were to send in their answers. At this adjourned meeting it was found that there was an almost unanimous vote in favor of union. So, amid thanksgiving to God for his goodness, and hearty demonstrations of joy on every hand, the two bodies whicl had been separated for more than thirty years again became one.

The principles and polity of the American branch of the Presbyterian church are similar to those of the church of Scotland. Each individual congregation is regarded, not as isolated and independent, but as connected, through its pastor and elders, with a large body, to which it is responsible. Acting on this principle, the Presbytery is constituted a court of review and control over all the churches in a certain district, and is composed of all the ministers and one ruling elder from every church within its bounds. The Synod is a higher court, reviewing the action of the several Presbyteries of which it is composed, and is formed of all the ministers and one elder from each church within its limits. The General Assembly is the highest judicatory, and the court of final appeal. It is formed yearly by a fair representation of ministers and elders from every Presbytery, and has a general supervision and control over the whole church. Within its bounds are twenty-eight Synods, one hundred and forty-six Presbyteries, and nearly three thousand churches. These are planted not only over our own nation, but are shedding their light amid the gloom of heathen superstition. They are scattered along our northern frontiers, while also a

Synod, composed of four Presbyteries and fifty churches, is found in our most southern borders. And while reports come to the Assembly from the Synod of the Pacific, the same body listens to similar accounts of spiritual progress from the Synod of Northern India, and from the Presbyteries of Canton and Ningpo, in the vast empire of China. Thus may it be said of the Presbyterian church, that upon her congregations and ministers the sun never sets.

The General Assembly has under its care and direction four theological seminaries. It also has divided its benevolent efforts into four great agencies, each of which is committed to a special Board of Managers. The Board of Foreign Missions has the care of the foreign field of missionary effort, having the supervision of stations among the Indian tribes of our own country, upon the western coast of Africa, in India, Siam, China, among the Jews, and in several Roman Catholic countries.

The Board of Domestic Missions attends to the supply of destitute places, and to the aid of feeble churches in our own country. The Board of Education has the whole field of the religious training of the young, and the preparation of candidates for the holy ministry. The Board of Publication attends to the isssuing of religious books and periodicals, providing volumes for the libraries of Sabbath-schools, and for family reading, together with tracts and papers for circulation by means of colporteurs. These various Boards are not irresponsible bodies, but are compelled to render yearly a strict and full account to the church, through its highest court, the General Assembly.

Here all their proceedings are considered, and any member of the body has the right to seek from their officers any information respecting their operations, or to suggest any changes therein. The history of the church since its present policy was completed, has fully shown the propriety and usefulness of its arrangements. The providence of God had evidently indicated that the time had come for it to enter the great field of Christian effort, not depending upon other churches for aid and co-operation, but with strong faith in God, and with earnest desires for his glory, to go forth and labour for the upbuilding of his kingdom, by the use of the means which he has appointed. Thus it now appears as a missionary church, and by the divine blessing it has been enabled to extend its bounds on the right hand and on the left, in our own land and among the nations that have long sat in darkness, lengthening its cords and strengthening its stakes, and enjoying indisputable evidence of the presence of Him who is the glory and strength of his church.

We have thus presented some of the leading features in the history of the Presbyterian church. It is no creation of modern reformers, appearing for the first time amid the convulsions which marked the era when Luther awoke the world from the sleep of ages. That great event but *restored* to the church its original form and order, by shaking off the corruptions which had marred its beauty and purity. The great and vital features of the Presbyterian system are as old as the church itself.

We have traced those principles in the records of the early Christian communities established by the apostles, and resembling the popular government of the Jewish synagogue. We have followed them as they retired with the persecuted people of God to the valleys of Piedmont, as they shone out even amid the darkness and corruptions of the Papacy in Scotland, Ireland and England, and as at the Reformation they fully and thoroughly revived amid the churches of continental Europe, and were sustained in Scotland even at the expense of suffering and death, against all the determined efforts of a proud and ambitious prelacy.

We have seen them early taking root in the New World, and spreading rapidly under the influences of earnest and faithful ministers of the word, until the church, with the divine blessing, has extended its institutions over our land, and is nobly engaged in fulfilling the last command of the ascending Saviour, "Go, preach my gospel to every creature."

There is much in the history of that church which serves to attach us warmly and zealously to it. Even the trials through which it has passed, the scenes of blood, and fire, and persecution through which it has been called to make its way, endear it to our hearts. Who can read the painful history of the Waldenses, and not admire the heroic courage and the unyielding constancy with which they contended for the faith once delivered to the saints. Who can trace the history of the church of Scotland, from the hour that it shook off the corruptions of Popery, through all the scenes of its earnest contests for the truth, down to the act that sundered it from the embraces of the State, and not feel that principles and doctrines which could lead to such earnestness and self-sacrifice are indeed noble, and could only have had their origin in the word and Spirit of God? Well may we love that church. It has been the home of martyrs and glorious witnesses for the truth, who, amid the fastnesses of the mountains, amid sufferings, and wrong, and outrage, amid prisons and at the stake, have testified to their undying adherence to its doctrines and order.

Nor do we feel less reverence for it, when we remember how nobly it has always sustained civil liberty. Notwithstanding all the clamour which has sometimes been raised against that church for a few isolated acts of severity, which were only individual acts, and more in self-defence than in a spirit of persecution, it is undeniable that it has ever been *the firm friend of civil freedom.* I need but point to the significant fact, that in those countries where Presbyterian principles prevail, there is the most liberal government. Holland was almost a model republic when the Puritans fled thither from the persecutions of the English prelacy. Geneva, Piedmont and Switzerland were far in advance of other nations of Europe, as to the freedom of their civil institutions, when the Reformation had fully restored their church to its Presbyterian and primitive character. Scotland could never be so wholly brought under the power of England, as to receive at her dictation that form of church government which best suited the pomp and pride of a royal court. Her sons have ever been free, since they were emancipated by the truth, and to maintain that liberty they have freely shed their blood. America, in the great struggle which separated her from despotism, found her most faithful friends amid the pastors and people of the Presbyterian church. Their prayers were offered and their treasure and blood poured forth for the success of that Revolution, which resulted in giving liberty a home upon the shores of the western world. Well may we love a church which has ever been identified with the dearest rights and the noblest blessings that man can enjoy.

And yet these facts are but the results of one yet more important, the *undeviating attachment of the church to the pure doctrines of the gospel.* In all its history, the truths of God's word have been held up as of far more importance, than the mere external forms of religion. In the primitive church it was enjoined upon its ministers to contend earnestly for the faith. In later ages the Waldenses bore a noble testimony for the truth, and when the church at the Reformation shook off the errors of the Papacy, it revived the doctrines of the gospel. Confessions of Faitth were published, embracing a full view of the cardinal truths of revelation, and those truths were held up as the means of salvation, and were made prominent as the source of spiritual life and health. It is for this that we love the Presbyterian church, and desire earnestly its prosperity, and rejoice in all the abundant tokens it has received of the presence and love of Him whose favour is the life and strength of his people. And how widely are its principles and order extended over the world! The Sabbath light that is dawning upon the churches of America, has just faded from lands where, in a language strange to us, but familiar in the ear of our common Father and God, the ministers of Jesus, ordained to their work after the manner of the apostles, by the laying on of the hands of the Presbytery, have been preaching the pure doctrines of the gospel. Under that same light the Waldensian pastors, amid their mountain homes, have borne new witness to the truth, and the churches of Holland have met for the worship of God, and the valleys of Switzerland and France have sheltered many a congregation who have listened to the truths which once were proclaimed by Calvin, and Le Fevre, and Beza, and Viret.

As the light of that blessed day has rolled on towards the west, it has found in Ireland many a warm and zealous worshipper, receiving the ordinances of the gospel from those who have been set apart to their work by Presbyters, whose apostolic authority none can deny, while in Scotland, her noble sons have listened to blessed instructions from the word of life, such as Knox once proclaimed, and the Covenanters heard amid secluded valleys, or upon the wild mountains, when seeking refuge from cruel persecutors. Thus may it be until the end shall come. Thus may our church enlarge the place of her habitation, and firmly holding the truth, and seeking to give it to all nations, enjoy the presence and love of Him whose promise is, "Lo, I am with you alway, even unto the end of the world."

APPENDIX.

NOTE A.

THE Confession of Faith of the Waldenses, found in a manuscript dated A. D. 1120, will show how nearly in doctrine they correspond with our own church.

A Confession of Faith of the Waldenses, bearing date A. D. 1120, *taken from the Cambridge MSS.*

"Article I.—We believe and firmly hold all that which is contained in the twelve articles of the symbol, which is called the Apostles' Creed, accounting for heresy whatsoever is disagreeing, and not consonant to the said twelve articles.

"Article II.—We do believe that there is one God, Father, Son, and Holy Spirit.

"Article III.—We acknowledge for the holy canonical Scriptures the books of the Holy Bible, viz:

"The Books of Moses, called Genesis, Exodus, Leviticus, Numbers, Deuteronomy, Joshua, Judges, Ruth, 1 Samuel, 2 Samuel, 1 Kings, 2 Kings, 1 Chronicles, 2 Chronicles, Ezra, Nehemiah, Esther, Job, Psalms, the Proverbs of Solomon, Ecclesiastes, or the Preacher, the Song of Solomon, the Prophecies of Isaiah and Jeremiah, the Lam entations of Jeremiah, Ezekiel, Daniel, Hosea, Joel, Amos, Obadiah, Jonas, Micah, Nahum, Habakkuk, Zephaniah, Haggai, Zechariah, Malachi.

"Here follow the books Apocryphal, which are not received of the Hebrews. But we read them (as saith St. Jerome in his Prologue to the Proverbs) for the instruction of the people, not to confirm the authority of the doctrines of the church, viz:

"Esdras, Tobit, Judith, Wisdom, Ecclesiasticus, Baruch with the Epistle of Jeremiah, Esther from the tenth chapter to the end, the Song of the Three Children in the Furnace, the History of Susannah, the History of the Dragon, 1 Maccabees, 2 Maccabees.

"Here follow the books of the New Testament:—

"The Gospel according to Sts. Matthew, Mark, Luke, John, the Acts of the Apostles, the Epistles of St. Paul to the Romans, 1 Corinthians, 2 Corinthians, Galatians, Ephesians, Philippians, Colossians, 1 Thessalonians, 2 Thessalonians, 1 Timothy, 2 Timothy, Titus, Philemon, the Epistle to the Hebrews, the Epistle of St. James, the first Epistle of St. Peter, the second Epistle of St. Peter, the first Epistle of St. John, the second Epistle of St. John, the third Epistle of St. John, the epistle of St. Jude, the Revelation of St. John.

"Article IV.—The books above said teach this, that there is one God, Almighty, all-wise and all-good, who has made all things by his goodness; for he formed Adam in his own image and likeness, but that by the envy of the devil, and the disobedience of the said Adam, sin has entered into the world, and that we are sinners in Adam and by Adam.

"Article V.—That Christ was promised to our fathers who received the law, that so knowing by the law their sin, unrighteousness and insufficiency, they might desire the coming of Christ, to satisfy for their sins, and accomplish the law by himself.

"Article VI.—That Christ was born in the time appointed by God the Father. That is to say, in the time when all iniquity abounded, and not for the cause of good works, for all were sinners; but that he might show us grace and mercy, as being faithful.

"Article VII.—That Christ is our life, truth, peace, and righteousness, also our pastor, advocate, sacrifice, and priest, who died for the salvation of all those that believe, and is risen for our justification.

"Article VIII.—In like manner, we firmly hold, that there is no other mediator and advocate with God the Father, save only Jesus Christ. And as for the Virgin Mary, that she was holy, humble, and full of grace; and in like manner do we believe concerning all the other saints, viz: that being in heaven, they wait for the resurrection of their bodies at the day of judgment.

"Article IX.—*Item*, we believe that after this life, there are only two places, the one for the saved, and the other for the damned, the which two places we call paradise and hell, absolutely denying that purgatory invented by antichrist, and forged contrary to the truth.

"Article X.—*Item*, we have always accounted as an unspeakable abomination before God, all those inventions of men, namely, the feasts and the vigils of saints, the water which they call holy; as likewise to abstain from flesh upon certain days, and the like; but especially their masses.

"Article XI.—We esteem for an abomination and as antichristian, all those human inventions which are a trouble or prejudice to the liberty of the spirit.

"Article XII.—We do believe that the sacraments are signs of the holy thing, or visible forms of the invisible grace, accounting it good that the faithful sometimes use the said signs or visible forms, if it may be done. However, we believe and hold, that the above said faithful may be saved without receiving the signs aforesaid, in case they have no place nor any means to use them.

"Article XIII.—We acknowledge no other sacraments but Baptism and the Lord's Supper.

"Article XIV.—We ought to honour the secular powers by submission, ready obedience, and paying of tributes."

Note B.

The following extracts, from the ancient discipline of the evangelical churches of the valleys of Piedmont, dated A. D. 1120, will show conclusively that the Presbyterian order and doctrine did not, as some affirm, originate with Calvin at the Reformation, but existed ages before, amid the living witnesses of the truth.

CONCERNING PASTORS.

"All those who are to be received as pastors among us, while they remain with their relations, entreat us to receive them into the ministry, as likewise that they would be pleased to pray God that they may be made worthy of so great a charge; but the said petitioners present such supplications to give a proof of their humility.

"We also appoint them their lessons, and set them to get by heart all the chapters of St. Matthew and St. John, with all the Epistles called canonical, and a good part of the writings of Solomon, David, and the prophets.

"And afterwards having good testimonials, they are by the imposition of hands admitted to the office of preaching.

"He that is last received ought to do nothing without the license of him that was received before him; and in like manner the former ought to do nothing without the license of his associate, to the end that all things among us may be done in good order.

"Our food and clothing are administered unto us, and given gratuitously, and by way of alms by the good people whom we instruct.

"Among the other powers which God hath given to his servants, he hath given them authority to elect the leaders who govern the people, and to constitute the elders in their charges, according to the diversity of the work in the unity of Christ, which is proved by the saying of the Apostle in the epistle to Titus, in chap. i., 'For this cause left I thee in Crete, that thou shouldst set in order the things that are wanting, and ordain elders in every city, as I had appointed thee.'

"When any of us, the aforesaid pastors, fall into any gross sin, he is both excommunicated and prohibited from preaching.

CONCERNING ELDERS, THE COLLECTIONS, AND COUNCILS.

"Rulers and elders are chosen out of the people, according to the diversity of the work, in the unity of Christ. And the Apostle proveth it to Titus, chap. i., 'For this cause left I thee in Crete, that thou shouldst set in order the things that are wanting, and ordain elders in every city, as I had appointed thee.'

"The money which is given us by the people, is by us carried to the aforesaid general council, and there delivered publicly in the presence of all; and afterwards the same is taken and distributed by our stewards; part of the money being given to such as are sent upon journeys for the occasion, and part of it given to the poor.

"We that are pastors assemble once a year to treat of our affairs in a general council."

NOTE C.

The Waldensian churches have ever paid great attention to the early instruction of their children. A Catechism was drawn up for this purpose, in the thirteenth century, from which the following is an extract:

Catechism of the Ancient Waldenses for the Instruction of their Youth, composed in the 13th century.

Minister. If one should demand of you, who you are, what would you answer?

Child. A creature of God, reasonable and mortal.

Min. Why has God created you?

Ans. To the end that I might know him and serve him, and be saved by his grace.

Min. Wherein consists your salvation?

Ans. In three substantial virtues, which necessarily belong to salvation.

Min. Which are they?

Ans. Faith, hope and charity.

Min. How can you prove that?

Ans. The apostle writes, 1 Cor. xiii., "Now abideth faith, hope and charity, these three."

Min. What is faith?

Ans. According to the apostle, Heb. xi., "It is the substance of things hoped for, and the evidence of things not seen."

Min. How many sorts of faith are there?

Ans. There are two sorts, viz., a living and a dead faith.

Min. What is a living faith?

Ans. It is that which works by charity.

Min. What is a dead faith?

Ans. According to St. James, it is that which without works is dead. Again, faith is null without works; or a dead faith is to believe that there is a God, and not to believe in him.

Min. What is your faith?

Ans. The true catholic and apostolic faith.

Min. What is that?

Ans. It in that which in the result (or symbol) of the apostles, is divided into twelve articles.

Min. What is that?

Ans. I believe in God the Father Almighty, &c.

Min. By what way can you know that you believe in God?

Ans. By this, that I know and I observe the commandments of God.

Min. How many commandments of God are there?

Ans. Ten, as is manifest in Exodus and Deuteronomy.

Min. Which are they?

Ans. "Hear, O Israel, I am the Lord thy God: thou shalt have none other gods before me. Thou shalt not make any graven image, or any likeness of any thing that is in heaven, &c."

Min. What is the sum or drift of these commandments?

Ans. It consists in these two great commandments, viz., Thou shalt love God above all things, and thy neighbour as thyself.

Min. What is that foundation of these commandments, by which every one may enter into life, and without which foundation none can do anything worthily, or fulfil the commandments?

Ans. The Lord Jesus Christ, of whom the apostle speaks in the 1 Cor., "Other foundation can no man lay, than that is laid, which is Jesus Christ."

Min. By what means may a man come to this foundation?

Ans. By faith, as saith St. Peter, 1 Pet. ii. 6, "Behold, I lay in Sion a chief corner-stone, elect, precious, and he that believeth on him shall not be confounded." And the Lord saith, "He that believeth hath eternal life."

Min. Whereby canst thou know that thou believest?

Ans. By this, that I know him to be true God, and true man, who was born, and who hath suffered, &c., for my redemption, justification, and that I love him, and desire to fulfil his commandments.

Min. By what means may one attain to those essential virtues, faith, hope, and charity?

Ans. By the gifts of the Holy Spirit.

Min. Dost thou believe in the Holy Spirit?

Ans. Yes, I do believe. For the Holy Spirit proceeds from the Father and the Son; and is one Person of the Trinity; and according to the Divinity, is equal to the Father and the Son.

Min. Thou believest God the Father, God the Son, and God the Holy Spirit; thou hast therefore three Gods.

Ans. I have not three.

Min. Yea, but thou hast named three.

Ans. That is by reason of the difference of the Persons, not by reason of the essence of the divinity. For although there are three Persons, yet notwithstanding there is but one essence.

NOTE D.

The following description of the parting interview between Calvin and his friends at Geneva, possesses an abiding interest. It has formed the subject of a painting of great merit by Herming, an artist of the city of Calvin:

"Conscious that his career was now fast drawing to a close, Calvin sent to inform the Syndics, and the other members of the Senate of Geneva, that he desired to address to them a few parting words, and that he hoped to be carried to their Hall for this purpose on the morrow. They begged that he would have regard to what his health would bear, and promised to attend him at his own house. When they had accordingly met (March 27th) he proceeded to address them. He had, he said, for some time been anxious to convey to them a few words of counsel and admonition, but that he had chosen to defer doing so till he had a sure foresight of his approaching dissolution. After thanking them for the great kindness he had experienced from them, for the honours they had conferred upon him, and for the forbearance which they had exercised towards his infirmities, he was bound to acknowledge, he said, that it had pleased God to employ him in rendering them some service, but he was conscious of his many deficiencies. Wherein he had come short he hoped they would forgive him, and impute it to his want of ability, rather than to his want of will to serve them; with respect, however, to his doctrine, he could solemnly declare that he had not taught rashly and uncertainly, but had delivered in all its purity and with sincerity the word of God; and this, he continued, 'I am the more anxious to testify, because I cannot doubt that Satan, as his practice is, will raise up heady, light-minded, ungodly men, to corrupt the sound doctrine which you have heard from me.' Then rapidly glancing at the dangers through which the infant republic had passed, and reminding them that it is God alone who can give stability to kingdoms, he continued: 'If you would have this republic continue in security, see to it that the sacred seat of authority in which God has placed you be not defiled with sin; for *them that honour him, he will honour; but they that despise him shall be lightly esteemed*. . . . I know,' he proceeded, 'the tempers and manners of you all, and I feel that you need exhortation. Let each one look to himself, and what he finds wanting in him let him ask of God. . . . I admonish the elders not to despise their juniors, and I warn the younger persons to conduct themselves with modesty, and to watch against presumption. . . . Resist every sinister aim and selfish affection; regard Him who has placed you in your station of honour, and seek the direction of his Holy Spirit.'

"To the ministers under the jurisdiction of Geneva, who likewise came to him, he said, 'Stand fast, my brethren, in the work on which you have entered, and let not your hearts fail you, for the Lord will preserve this church and republic against all its enemies. Far from you be all discords among yourselves; embrace one another in mutual charity.' Then, alluding to the precarious state of the church, threatened by enemies both from without and within, and encouraging them to perseverance by relating some of his own experiences, he continued, 'Do you, therefore, also persist in your vocation: uphold the established order; and see that the people be at the same time retained in obedience to the doctrine delivered unto them, for some are yet wicked and contumacious. . . . I avow that I have lived united with you, brethren, in the strictest bonds of true and sincere affection; and I take my leave of you with the same feelings. If you have at any time found me harsh or peevish under mine afflictions, I entreat your forgiveness. Farewell!' He then shook hands with them all, and 'we took leave of him,' says Beza, 'with sad hearts, and by no means with dry eyes—parting with him as from a common parent.'"

Note E.

The following interesting notices of the present state of the Waldensian church, are from the report of Rev. J. P. Revel, Moderator of the Waldensian Synod, in the year 1853, whose visit to this country will long be remembered with pleasure. The report appears in the Foreign Missionary of July, 1854.

"I. *Parishes.*—There are fifteen. At the head of each there is a pastor, and a presbytery or consistory presided over by him, consisting of several elders—from four to twelve. The Vaudois population is about twenty-three thousand souls. There is one pastor emeritus, of the age of eighty years, and there are four widows of pastors, for whom an annual contribution from all the pastors in active service makes a small pension. Five candidates have received the laying on of hands; three are employed in the Italian mission, of whom one, De Sanctis, was formerly curé of the parish of the Magdalen at Rome, and a member of the Holy Office; one is a pastor of a parish; and the fifth is a professor in the College.

"II. *Schools.*—There are sixteen principal schools, whose teachers are furnished with a commission [brevet]; fourteen girls' schools, and one hundred and forty-five schools in hamlets, during the four winter months. The whole number of scholars, according to the reports lately received, is four thousand seven hundred and ninety-two.

"III. *College.*—Eight professors are teaching the elements of the Latin, French and Italian languages to children of nine or ten years of age; also in the higher mathematics, the natural sciences and philosophy to young people of eighteen or twenty years of age. The number of scholars is eighty-four, in nine classes, in each of which they spend a year.

"A Normal School has been established within two years. It prepares teachers, colporteurs, and evangelists. It has twenty-four students, who give great satisfaction. Most of them are poor; they make sacrifices in order to learn. Some assistance was procured for them the last winter, provisions being so high; many of them seldom have enough to eat.

"In a school for young ladies, twelve pupils have received lessons from college professors and from a female teacher, who also instructs them in domestic labours.

"IV. *The Poor.*—A hospital with twenty-five beds receives the sick poor attacked with curable maladies. A deaconess has charge of the in-door services. A deaconess in each parish collects and distributes charity to the most needy. This year provisions have been so dear, that many of our poor would have suffered, if some English friends had not sent us $1400, to assist the most destitute.

"*Orphan Asylum.*—The need of a place of refuge for poor and deserted orphans has been long felt, and this winter more than ever. Two friends enabled Mrs. Revel to arrange with an excellent Christian woman to receive six little girls; now there are eight. When one compares their present circumstances with their former condition, he sees that a good work has been commenced.

"V. *Italian Mission.*—This part of the work of our church ought to be performed with zeal, prudence and vigour, upon pain of failing in the end for which God has so wonderfully preserved this church. The Lord has been pleased moreover to stimulate us by remarkable success. Six missionary stations formed in the Sardinian states in four years, show that the church considers it her duty to accomplish this work. She employs at these six stations the following number of labourers: (1) at *Pignerol*, a clerical (consacré) evangelist, and occasionally a lecturer and a colporteur; (2) at *Turin*, two clerical evangelists, two colporteurs, and latterly a master and mistress of a school, and an evangelist not ordained; (3) at *Cazale*, a lay evangelist; (4) at *Genes*, four evangelists, of whom one is ordained, and two colporteurs; (5) at *Favale*, a lay evangelist, who also has a school; (6) at *Nice*, three evangelists, of whom two are clerical, and two colporteurs. We have also an evangelist at Constantinople, where there is a large Italian population.

"VI. *Divers Facts.*—A fine Protestant church was opened at Turin, on the 20th of October.

This is a real event in the extension of the kingdom of God in Italy. Shortly afterwards we purchased at Genes an old Catholic church, secularized in 1808. The archbishop and the priests stirred up various manœuvres before the court and government [to prevent this]; by considerations of public tranquillity they would have hindered us from preaching the gospel where they had chanted mass. In the meantime, a spiritual church was built up at Genes; we were blessed of God. We expect soon to build houses of prayer at Nice and at Pignerol. Some friends in England have remitted the funds necessary for building at the former place; and we have received from America the funds required for the latter."

NOTE F.

The following extract, from D'Aubigné's "Germany, England and Scotland," gives a touching record of the sufferings endured by ministers of the Free Church at the disruption:

"Many of them sacrificed all they had, even all of their living. The amount of the revenue was more than a hundred thousand pounds, which these brethren joyfully relinquished for the sake of Him who has said, 'Every one that hath forsaken houses, or brethren, or sisters, or father, or mother or wife, or children, or lands, for my sake, shall receive an hundred fold, and shall inherit everlasting life.' (Matthew xix. 29.) No one swerved; old and young alike traced, with a determined hand, the few strokes which signed away their all. The execution of this act occupied five hours, and during that time the Assembly remained in silent emotion, watching with respect the devotion of their leaders. Four hundred and seventy-four ministers resigned their benefices, either then or shortly afterwards; about two thousand elders adhered to the act. Both numbers united formed the majority of the office bearers of the church. The majority of the church members, in full communion, was also ranged on the side of liberty.

"Such was the disruption and the creation of the Free Church. But the sacrifice then accomplished in the Hall of Tanfield was not the greatest. The ministers had to return to the mountains, to the plains, even to the remotest shores of Scotland, to bring their wives and children from their homes. The hour was at hand when Jesus was to say in every manse, 'If any man will come after me let him deny himself, and take up his cross and follow me.' (Matt. xvi. 24.) Hundreds in Scotland were then fulfilling this Christian duty, and taking the cross upon their shoulders, were ready to exclaim, 'Lord, here am I!' How many scenes were there enacting, enough to break the hardest heart!

"In a certain part of the country, two ministers were conversing a short time before the disruption. 'Do you think there is no chance of a settlement?' said the minister of the place to his friend. 'We are as certain of being out, as that the sun will rise to-morrow,' replied the other. A groan was heard; it came from the very heart of the mother of the family; they had had many trials in their day. There had been cradles and coffins in their home, and the place was endeared to the mother by many associations; there was not a flower, or a shrub, or a tree, that was not dear to her; some of them were planted by the hands of those who were in their graves, and that poor woman's heart was like to burst. But grace was mightier than nature, and when the day of trial arrived, she came forth as readily as her husband, although it was breaking her very heart-strings to leave a home where she had expected to breathe her last, and to be laid in the churchyard, among the ashes of her children.

"In another instance, there was a venerable mother in Christ, who had gone to the place in the days of her youth, when it was a wilderness, but who, with her husband, had turned it into an Eden. Her husband had died there. Her son was now its minister. That venerable widow and mother, like Anna, the daughter of Phanuel, had seen the snows and sorrows of eighty years accumulate upon her head, and like an aged tree, which has fixed its roots deeply in the ground, she was attached to this home of her youth by the dearest affections. All her anxieties, her prayers to God, were for two things: either that the church should come to a right settlement with the State; or, if that should fail, that then her son should do his duty. The disruption came; all was to be given up, and this venerable mother in Israel was the first to go forth; and she found in her new home, by the blessing of Christ, more health and happiness than she had enjoyed for a long time before. Some time ago, a minister was walking by moonlight with another, Mr Guthrie, who is restoring manses to the servants of God throughout Scotland. The two companions were passing before the beloved home which the former of them had left for the cause of truth. No light shone from the house; no smoke rose above the roof. Pointing to it in the moonlight, Mr. G. said, 'Oh, my friend, it was a noble thing to leave that house.' 'Ah, yes,' he replied, 'it was a noble thing; but for all that it was a bitter thing. I shall never forget the night I left that house till I am laid in my grave. When I saw my wife and children go forth in the gloaming—when I saw them for the last time leave our own door, and when in the dark I was left alone, with none but God, in that house, and when I had to take water and quench the fire on my own hearth, and put out the candle in my own house, and turn the key against myself and my wife and my little ones. That night—God in his mercy grant that such a night I may never see again! It was a noble thing to leave the manse, and I bless God for the grace which was given to me; but for all that, it was a cruel and bitter night to me.' In another place, in the Highlands, when the last evening had arrived, a poor minister had placed his wife and children in a rough cart, and walking behind them, began to cross the mountains. A heavy snow storm was then raging on that elevated spot. The mountain was white, although it was summer time, and the sky was dark. The poor family went on amidst the driving snow and cutting wind. 'We knew not where to find a place to dwell in,' said the minister, 'but never did I know so much of the peace of God as I did that night.' Thus are fulfilled the Saviour's precious promises: The Lord is my Shepherd, I shall not want.'"

Note G.

The following description of the ordinary proceedings of the Assembly is given by Robert Baillie, who was a member of that body from Scotland:

"The like of that Assembly I did never see, and as we hear say, the like was never in England, nor anywhere is shortly like to be. They did sit in Henry the 7th Chapel, in the place of the Convocation; but since the weather grew cold, they did go to the Jerusalem Chamber, a fair room in the Abbey of Westminster, about the size of the college front hall, but wider. At the one end nearest the door, and along both sides, are stages of seats, as in the new Assembly house at Edinburgh, but not so high, for there will be room for five or six score. At the uppermost end there is a chair set on a frame, a foot from the earth, for the Mr. Prolocutor, Dr. Twisse. Before it, on the ground, stand two chairs for the two Mr. Assessors, Dr. Burgess and Mr. White. Before these two chairs, through the length of the room, stands a table, at which sit the two Scribes, Mr. Byfield and Mr. Roborough. The house is all well hung (with tapestry), and has a good fire, which is some dainties at London. Opposite the table, upon the Prolocutor's right hand, there are three or four ranks of benches. On the lowest we five do sit. Upon the other, at our backs, the members of

Parliament deputed to the Assembly. On the benches opposite us, on the prolocutor's left hand, going from the upper end of the house to the chimney, and at the other end of the house and back of the table, till it come about to our seats, are four or five stages of benches, upon which the divines sit as they please; albeit commonly they keep the same place. From the chimney to the door there are no seats, but a void space for passage. The lords of the Parliament used to sit on chairs, in that void about the fire. We meet every day of the week but Saturday. We sit commonly from nine till one or two, afternoon. The prolocutor, at the beginning and end, has a short prayer. The man, as the world knows, is very learned in the questions he has studied, and very good, beloved of all and highly esteemed; but merely bookish, not much, as it seems, acquainted with conceived prayer, and among the unfittest of all the company for any action; so after the prayer he sits mute. It was the canny convoyance (skilful management) of those who guide most matters for their own interest to plant such a man, of purpose, in the chair. The one Assessor, our good friend, Mr. White, has keeped in of the gout since our coming; the other, Dr. Burgess, a very active and sharp man, supplies, so far as is decent, the prolocutor's place. Ordinarily there will be present above three score of their divines.

"These are divided into three committees, in one of which every man is a member. No man is excluded who pleases to come to any of the three. Every committee, as the Parliament gives order in writing to take any purpose to consideration, takes a portion, and in their afternoon meetings, prepares matters for the Assembly, and sets down their minds in distinct propositions with texts of Scripture. After the prayer, Mr. Byfield, the scribe, reads the proposition and Scriptures, whereupon the Assembly debates in a most grave and orderly way. No man is called up to speak; but whosoever stands up of his own accord, speaks so long as he will without interruption. If two or three stand up at once, then the divines confusedly call on his name whom they desire to hear first; on whom the loudest and manifest voices call, he speaks. No man speaks to any but the prolocutor. They harangue long and very learnedlie. They study the questions well before hand, and prepare their speeches; but withal the men are exceeding prompt and well spoken. I do marvel at the very accurate and extemporal replies that many of them usually make. When upon every proposition by itself, and on every text of Scripture that is brought to confirm it, every man who will has said his whole mind, and the replies, duplies and triplies are heard, then the most part call, 'To the question.' Byfield, the scribe, rises from the table and comes to the prolocutor's chair, who, from the scribe's book, reads the proposition, and says, 'As many as are of opinion that the question is well stated in the proposition, let them say, Aye.' When Aye is heard he says, 'As many as think otherwise, say No.' If the difference of Ayes and Noes be clear, as usually it is, then the question is ordered by the scribes, and they go on to debate the first Scripture alleged for proof of the proposition. If the sound of Aye and No be near equal, then says the prolocutor, 'As many as say Aye stand up;' while they stand, the scribe and others number them in their minds; when they sit down, the Noes are bidden to stand, and they, likewise, are numbered. This way is clear enough, and saves a great deal of time, which we spend in reading our catalogue. When a question is once ordered, there is no more debate of that matter; but if a man will wander from his subject, he is quickly taken up by Mr. Assessor, or many others, confusedly crying, 'Speak to order, to order.' No man contradicts another expressly by name, but most discreetly speaks to the prolocutor, and at most holds to general terms: 'The reverend brother who lately, or last, spoke on this hand, on that side, above, or below.'

"I thought meet once for all to give you a taste of the outward form of their Assembly. They follow the way of their Parliament. Much of their way is good, and worthy of our imitation; only their longsomeness is woeful at this time, when their church and kingdom lie under a most lamentable anarchy and confusion. They see the hurt of their length, but cannot get it helped; for being to establish a new platform of worship and discipline to their nation for all time to come, they think they cannot be answerable if solidly, and at leisure, they do not examine every point thereof."

Note H.

The following articles, adopted by the Elders and Messengers of the churches, assembled in Synod at Cambridge, 1648, will show how nearly the early ministers of New England assimilated in their views of church order to those of Presbyterians.

CHAPTER VII—OF RULING ELDERS AND DEACONS.

"I. The ruling elders' office is distinct from the office of pastor and teacher. The ruling elders are not so called to exclude the pastors and teachers from ruling, because ruling and governing is common to these with the other; whereas, to teach and preach the word is peculiar to the former.

"II. The ruling elders' work is to join with the pastor, in those acts of spiritual rule, which are distinct from the ministry of the word and sacraments committed to them, of which sort these be as followeth:

"1. To open and shut the doors of God's house, by the admission of members approved by the church, and by the excommunication of notorious and obstinate offenders renounced by the church. 5. To be guides and leaders to the church in all whatsoever, pertaining to church administration and actions. 8. To feed the flock of God with a word of admonition; 9. and as they shall be sent for, to visit and to pray over their sick brethren; 10. and at other times as opportunity shall serve thereunto.

"III. The office of a deacon is instituted in the church by the Lord Jesus; sometimes they are called Helps. The office and work of a deacon, is to receive the offerings of the church, and to keep the treasury of the church, and therewith to serve the tables which the church is to provide for, as the Lord's table, the table of the ministers, and of such as are in necessity, to whom they are to distribute in their simplicity.

CHAPTER XVI—OF SYNODS.

"1. Synods orderly assembled, and rightly proceeding according to the pattern, Acts xv., we acnowledge as the ordinance of Christ.

"4. It belongeth unto Synods and Councils to debate and *determine* controversies of faith, and cases of conscience; to clear from the word holy directions for the holy worship of God and good government of the church; to bear witness against mal-administration and corruption in doctrine or manners in any particular church, and to give direction for the reformation thereof."

NOTE I.

THE REUNION movement may be said to have received its first active impulse during the late war for the Union, in which Christians of all denominations met and laboured together in the army for the spiritual welfare of the soldiers. A fraternal spirit was thus begotten, which increased and widened in its influence, until the question began to be asked whether there might not be closer bonds of union between brethren of different names, and whether there was any valid reason why the two great bodies of the Presbyterian family in America should any longer be separated.

In the year 1864, at the meeting of General Assembly (O. S.), in Newark, a paper looking toward Reunion was signed by seventy ministers and forty-three ruling elders. In the next year both Assemblies met at St. Louis, when the subject was again more openly discussed, and a committee from either branch was appointed to draft a basis of organic Reunion. The names of the Committee were as follows:

Old School.—John M. Krebs, D.D., Charles C. Beatty, D.D., John I. Backus, D.D., Phineas D. Gurley, D.D., Jos. G. Monfort, D.D., William D. Howard, D.D., Wm. E. Schenck, D.D., Villeroy D. Reed, D.D., and Frederick T. Brown, D.D., *Ministers;* James W. Ray, Hon. Robert McKnight, Hon. Samuel Galloway, Hon. Hovey K. Clark, Hon. George P. Strong and Prof. Ormond Beatty, *Ruling Elders.*

New School.—Thos. Brainerd, D.D., William Adams, D.D., Edwin F. Hatfield, D.D., Jonathan F. Stearns, D.D., Philemon H. Fowler, D.D., James B. Shaw, D.D., Henry L. Hitchcock, D.D., Robert W. Patterson, D.D., and Henry A. Nelson, D.D., *Ministers;* Hon. Edward A. Lambert, Hon. Joseph Allison, Hon. Henry W. Williams, Hon. Truman P. Handy, Robert W. Steele and Hon. Jacob S. Farrand, *Ruling Elders.*

In consequence of the death of two of the members, Drs. Krebs and Brainerd, their places were filled by J. E. Rockwell, D.D., and George F. Wiswell, D.D.

The first report of the committees was made to the Assemblies in the year 1867. It was accepted by both bodies, and ordered to be sent down to the Presbyteries for their consideration. In consequence of objections to the doctrinal basis, it was rejected by the Presbyteries of the Old School branch of the Church. The point of objection was the sentence concerning the reception of the Confession of Faith, which read, "And its fair historical sense, as it is accepted by the two bodies in opposition to Antinomianism and Fatalism on the one hand, and to Arminianism and Pelagianism on the other, shall be regarded as the sense in which it is received and adopted."

In the month of November, 1867, a large National Union Convention of Presbyterians was held in the city of Philadelphia, which gave a fresh impetus to the Reunion movement. Delegates from the four great branches of the Presbyterian family were present in considerable numbers, and a basis of Union was adopted which met with general approval. In the month of March, 1868, the committee of the two Assemblies again met at Philadelphia, and continued in session for nearly a week. The doctrinal basis was modified so as to meet if possible the views of all parties, as those views had been represented in the November Convention. The basis of Reunion was again sent down to the Presbyteries, and accepted by those of the New School, while a majority of the Old School voted against it, but expressed their willingness to unite on the basis of the standards, pure and simple. In the year 1869 both Assemblies met in New York, when a joint committee amended the articles of Reunion so as to meet the evident demands of the Church. These were sent down to the Presbyteries, who acted upon them at their fall meetings, and sent in their answers to the Assemblies, which had adjourned to meet at Pittsburg on the 10th of November, 1869.

Committees from either body announced to the

other the result of the vote. Each Assembly was formally dissolved, and a new one ordered to meet the next year in the First Church of Philadelphia, and then the two bodies came together. The New School body marched in double file down to the gate in front of the church, where it was met by the Old School Assembly, and the two bodies marched in parallel column for about a square. Here they halted, and Drs Jacobus and Fowler, the Moderators of the two Assemblies, and the other officers and members grasping hands united in one column and marched to the Third Church, which was now filled to its utmost capacity. Here they united in religious services and mutual congratulations and expressions of good will. A cable despatch announcing the grand result was sent to the Presbyterians of Great Britain and Ireland.

Addresses were made by the two Moderators and by Drs. Adams, Musgrave, Hall and Fisher, and by Elders Strong, Drake, Day and Dodge, members of the two Assemblies. Prayers were offered by Dr. Hatfield and Mr. Robert Carter, and then the Apostolic Benediction was pronounced by Rev. Dr. Jacobus. Thus was consummated this grand Reunion of the two great bodies of the American Presbyterian Church, after a separation of over thirty years.

www.ingramcontent.com/pod-product-compliance
Lightning Source LLC
LaVergne TN
LVHW010220110826
845151LV00004B/1157
9781425527563